DENMARK

BALTIC SEA

Barth
(Luft Stalag 1)

HAMBURG

BREMERHAVEN

Elbe River

Meppel
Staphorst

BERLIN

GERMANY

Merseburg

Rhine River

Oberursel (Dulag Luft)

FRANKFURT

PRAGUE

Front Line

NORTHWEST EUROPE
December 1944

BEHIND ENEMY LINES:
A YOUNG PILOT'S STORY

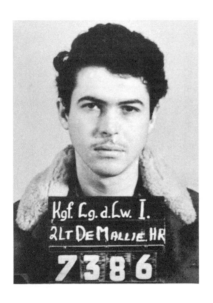

Prisoner of war picture of the author, Howard R. DeMallie

BEHIND ENEMY LINES: A YOUNG PILOT'S STORY

HOWARD R. DEMALLIE

STERLING PUBLISHING CO., INC.

New York

J
921
DE MALLIE

A FLYING POINT PRESS BOOK

Design: PlutoMedia
Front cover painting: Courtesy of the author
Back cover and frontispiece: Courtesy of the author

Library of Congress Cataloging-in-Publication Data

DeMallie, H. R. (Howard R.)
Behind enemy lines : a young pilot's story / Howard R. DeMallie. — Updated ed.
p. cm. — (Sterling Point books)
Prev. ed. published under the title: Beyond the dikes.
Includes index.
ISBN-13: 978-1-4027-4517-1 (trade)
ISBN-10: 1-4027-4517-6
ISBN-13: 978-1-4027-4137-1 (pbk.)
ISBN-10: 1-4027-4137-5
1. DeMallie, H. R. (Howard R.)—Juvenile literature. 2. World War, 1939-1945—Underground movements—Netherlands—Juvenile literature. 3. World War, 1939-1945—Prisoners and prisons, German—Juvenile literature. 4. World War, 1939-1945—Personal narratives, American—Juvenile literature. 5. Prisoners of war—United States—Biography—Juvenile literature. 6. Prisoners of war—Germany—Biography—Juvenile literature. I. DeMallie, H. R. (Howard R.). Beyond the dikes. II. Title.

D802.N4D44 2007
940.54'7243092—dc22
[B]
                            2006032134

          1   3   5   7   9   10   8   6   4   2

Published by Sterling Publishing Co., Inc.
387 Park Avenue South, New York, NY 10016
Original edition published by Dry Bones Press
under the title *Beyond the Dikes*
Copyright © 2000 by H. R. DeMallie
New material in this updated edition
Copyright © 2007 by Flying Point Press
Map and diagram copyright © by Richard Thompson, Creative Freelancers, Inc.
Distributed in Canada by Sterling Publishing
c/o Canadian Manda Group, 165 Dufferin Street
Toronto, Ontario, Canada M6K 3H6
Distributed in the United Kingdom by GMC Distribution Services
Castle Place, 166 High Street, Lewes, East Sussex, England BN7 1XU
Distributed in Australia by Capricorn Link (Australia) Pty. Ltd.
P. O. Box 704, Windsor, NSW 2756, Australia

Sterling ISBN-13: 978-1-4027-4517-1
ISBN-10: 1-4027-4517-6

For information about custom editions, special sales, premium and
corporate purchases, please contact Sterling Special Sales Department
at 800-805-5489 or specialsales@sterlingpub.com.

To my grandchildren

CONTENTS

CONTENTS

BEHIND ENEMY LINES:
A YOUNG PILOT'S STORY

INTRODUCTION

FOR MUCH OF WORLD WAR II ENGLAND WAS surrounded by enemy territory. The British army was defeated in France and driven back to England in the early days of the war. German bombers were conducting devastating raids against British cities. Nazi submarines were sinking hundreds of Allied ships trying to bring vital supplies to Britain. German armies loomed in occupied France just across the narrow English Channel. These were indeed desperate days for the Allies.

With no other choice, it fell to the air forces of Britain and the United States to conduct war in northern Europe.

Long before the D-Day invasion in June 1944, there were brave men from the United States and Britain fighting desperate, bloody battles against Germany in the skies over the continent.

They were the airmen who flew bombing raids over Germany. Their mission was to destroy the factories, oil refineries, ports, transportation systems, and depots that the Nazis used to supply their armed forces in the war against the Allies.

Before World War II broke out, the Germans had built up an enormous industrial capacity for building airplanes, tanks, ammunition, and submarines. They also built oil refineries to supply the fuel for their war machines. If the Allies were to have any chance at all against Hitler's vast armies, the air forces of Britain and the United States had to be successful in crippling his industries.

It was not an easy task. The Germans protected their factories with thousands of anti-aircraft guns. In addition, their own air force consisted of thousands of highly skilled pilots flying speedy, well-armed, state-of-the-art fighter planes that could be launched in an instant against the much slower bombers flying over from English airfields. Furthermore, England itself was a small island, surrounded by Nazi-held territory. The Germans knew exactly where the bombers were going to come from and they could lie in wait for them.

The task of sending bombers over Germany was split between the British and the Americans. The British would, under cover of night, use their Lancaster bombers to attack German targets. By day, it would be the Americans in their B-17 and B-24 bombers. The British bombers carried more bombs and fewer guns to protect them, thus operating at night was important. The Americans in their heavily protected B-17 bombers ventured out in daylight and thus were able to attack their targets with more precision. Even so, the B-17s were vulnerable to attack by fast German fighter planes. They suffered heavy losses, especially when they ventured deep into German territory. To offset these losses, the Mustang P-51 escort fighter was developed. It had the capability of accompanying the B-17s all the way to Berlin.

Nevertheless, the toll on Allied air forces was great.
Over 40,000 American and British planes were lost and
79,000 American airmen and a similar number of British
airmen were killed in action in the European air war.
What follows is the story of one of those B-17 bombers
and her crew.

The Editors

IT WAS A DECEMBER DAY, COLD, WITH NO HINT of warmth to be seen in the ragged gray of the sky above. A chilling breeze swept across the land, and ripples marred the surface of the water that now covered the once fertile fields. On somewhat higher ground an old man trudged along—his hands thrust deep in his pockets. The pain in his eyes was apparent as he surveyed the barren waste surrounding him. This was his land, his home, his Holland. It was hard to believe but the muddy turbulent seawater from the ruptured dikes was really there, covering everything, robbing the fields for years to come of any fertility. Yes, this was his Holland. No longer a Holland of green and fruitful fields and happy laughing people, but a land robbed of its goodness, filled with oppression and misery. This was German-occupied Holland of December 1944.

The man paused as an icy gust of wind tugged at his clothes. His mind was no longer on the scene before him, but intent on the sound that came with the wind. There it was again. It was louder now. And the man lifted his face to the sky as he could now detect the roar of engines. It was not a steady sound he heard, but one broken with snarling and cracking. Then through the haze of the overcast he saw the great ship come slipping toward the earth. Parachutes began to stream from the ship, and the man watched fascinated by the panorama enacted before him. Suddenly his gaze transformed to one of mute horror as he saw almost directly overhead a black speck resolve into a twisting tumbling body racing toward the earth. He watched unable to tear his eyes from the scene until the body disappeared behind a nearby cluster of trees. The sight was gone, but his ears echoed and re-echoed with the agonizing cry that came on the wind. The old man, sobbing, covered his face with his hands and was sick.

CHAPTER 1

ENLISTING
FOR ADVENTURE

I LOOKED UP AS ANOTHER B-24 LIBERATOR streaked across the blue Michigan sky. It was coming from the Ford plant at nearby Willow Run where they were in full production building bombers for the war.

Ever since 1939 when Germany invaded Poland, the newspapers had been full of disastrous news as Hitler invaded and then occupied France, Belgium, Holland, and little Luxembourg. England was being bombed night and day . . . how long could she hold out against the horrible aggression of Hitler's Third Reich?

Then on December 7, 1941 the Japanese had bombed

our airbase at Pearl Harbor, Hawaii. The next day President Roosevelt declared war.

And here I was, an engineering student at the University of Michigan—not a lot of adventure here in Ann Arbor. Maybe it was time for me to enlist. It would be great if my best friend Roy Brockman would enlist too.

I kept my eye on the Liberator. Every time I saw one I knew I wanted to fly. What would it be like to pilot one of those beauties? What would it feel like to dodge enemy flak on a bombing mission? Someone once said, "Young men enlist in the service during war time primarily for adventure."

Well then, it had to be the Army Air Force for me.

Roy and I set off together for basic training in Florida— hard work but pretty soon we were flying little planes and then bigger planes. We were eventually assigned to fly the B-17 bomber, the "Flying Fortress."

First, a word about this B-17 that we were learning to fly. It was called the "Flying Fortress" because not only did the plane carry as much as 10,000 pounds of bombs, it was also armed with as many as thirteen machine guns that were designed to protect the plane from enemy fighters when it was on a bombing mission.

The B-17 had four 1,200-horsepower engines that gave it a top speed of almost 300 miles per hour, though its normal cruising speed was 150 miles per hour. Over twelve thousand B-17s were built between 1935 and 1945. They were the most important bomber used by the American Army Air Force in World War II—especially in the war in Europe.

The B-17s crew consisted of nine or ten men. There were four officers—a pilot, a co-pilot, a navigator, and a bombardier. In addition, there were five or six enlisted men—an engineer, a radio operator, and three or four gunners.

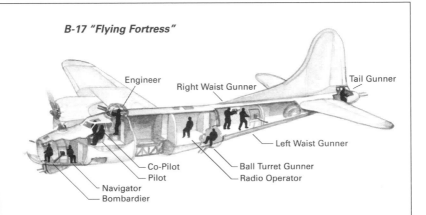

B-17 "Flying Fortress"

Pilot
The pilot is the commander of the airplane and is responsible for the safety and efficiency of the crew. The pilot sits on the left seat of the cockpit.

Co-Pilot
The co-pilot is the chief assistant and right arm of the pilot. He has to be familiar with all the duties of the pilot, in order to be able to take over if needed.

Navigator
The navigator must determine the exact position of the airplane at all times with the aid of instruments, radio navigation, or celestial navigation. The navigator also operates and services one of the machine guns located near his station.

Bombardier
The bombardier is responsible for aiming and dropping the airplane's bombs. He is in command of the plane during the bombing run. The bombardier also operates the machine guns located on the nose of the B-17.

Radio Operator
The radio operator is responsible for all the radio equipment of B-17. His duties include giving position reports and keeping the radio equipment in good operating order. He also acts as one of the gunners.

Engineer
The engineer knows all about how the airplane and all its equipment works. He checks engine operation, fuel consumption, and the operation of all equipment. The engineer usually operates the top turret guns.

Gunners
There are between eleven and thirteen 50 caliber machine guns on board the B-17. In addition to the radio operator, the engineer, the navigator, and the bombardier, there are three or four men whose only job is to operate the machine guns — particularly the waist guns on the sides of the airplane, the tail guns at the rear of the plane, and the ball turret guns on the underside of the airplane.

CHAPTER 2

TROOPSHIP TO ENGLAND

AFTER CHUCK OLSON, OUR NAVIGATOR, JOINED our crew we were at last "crewed-up"—ten proud B-17 "combat-to-be" crewmen. We were ready and eager to complete our training and get into the fight before the war was over.

Following graduation from flight school, we planned a real celebration—a crew banquet. A banquet with all the goodies we could afford. Actually, we planned more than one. We planned two. The first, we were to hold before we left on our journey to England, and the skies over Germany. The second was to be on our return. . . . How naive we were.

11

That first get-together was one of the last weekends we were in the States. We made the trip together from our air base to nearby Memphis, Tennessee. We picked up our current dates and then regrouped at the rooftop restaurant of the Hotel Peabody. It was a beautiful summer night and our banquet table was outside directly beneath the brightest of stars. The beauty of the night, the soft lights, the music of the orchestra, the happiness of the people around us made us both sentimental and hilarious with joy and pride. As I sat at the table, and glanced at those faces around me, everyone so strong and full of character, I couldn't keep a lump from rising in my throat. These were the Airmen who were entrusted to me, and I prayed to God that I would be worthy of being their "Skipper." The crew always called me "Skipper," the name almost every pilot is sure to be given by his crew. But, unconsciously, I would square my shoulders and hold my head a bit higher whenever I was so greeted. I was proud of these guys, and proud to be their leader.

Sitting at the far end of the table was my co-pilot, Dick

Fuller. I relied on Dick, and the mutual trust we built up between us developed into a close friendship. The two remaining officers in the crew were Bill Leader, my bombardier and Chuck, my navigator—all four of us, budding second lieutenants. The rest of the guys were the finest I could ever hope to have fly with me. The six of them, from "Pappy" Derr, the oldest (he was all of twenty-six) to Lowell Strain, the youngest (just nineteen) were hard-working, devil-may-care types, and I may have been biased, but I would have matched them with any crew at our operational training base.

When we had finished stuffing ourselves, Loel Bishop, the second youngest of the lot, scrambled awkwardly to his feet. His face was flushed with comradeship and happiness as he lifted his glass high over his head. "A toast," he cried, running his free hand through his tousled dark hair. "A toast to skipper—may he fly us high!" How corny can anyone get, but the boys rose to their feet and drank the toast while I, with an awkward grin on my face, tried to conceal my embarrassment and the lump in my throat. Then they went the rounds, toasting each other. Laughingly, jokingly, they managed to credit each his due with surprising exactness.

At last came my turn. I felt that something more was expected of me, and my thoughts ran wild, seeking fitting words. Slowly, rising to my feet, my mind still a perfect blank, I reached for my glass. "Here's to—" I paused, grasping for the correct words. (I had never made a serious toast or a speech before; gosh, I was only twenty-two years old.) Then out it came, "Here's to all of you," and I motioned to them with my glass. "All of you who make this crew of ours what it is—the best damned crew in the Air Corps. May you and I together—may we—take our ship into combat. May we do our best, and may we return victorious. I thank you, from the bottom of my heart, for your trust in me. I'll do my best to be worthy of it. From Dick in his seat beside me, to you 'Bish' way back in the tail, no pilot was ever given a better gang. Together I'm sure we will face danger, and by God together we will return. Drink to this all of you," I charged. "Drink to our crew." I put my glass to my lips and they rose and followed suit. And then with a surge of excitement, spurred on by the scene before me, and the fact that I had made what I thought was a pretty darn good speech, and that undoubtedly I had seen too many movies, and that I had too much to drink, I dashed my glass to the floor. The others followed suit, and that crash of glass and the spirit prompting it will never leave my mind. Ah! That was a night! In my mind I've lived it over many times, even the less than happy thought of my reimbursing the irate restaurant manager for the broken glasses.

Before we left we each received an eight-by-ten copy of a photograph that had been taken earlier as we sat around the table. Then after delivering our dates back to their respective homes, we had a jovial trip back to the base on the 3:30 A.M. bus, winding up our eventful evening.

Shortly after our crew banquet, we entered into the final stages of the operational training that prepared U.S. air combat crews for action in the ETO, the European Theater of Operations. In addition to intensive flight training we made practice bombing runs, had aerial gun-nery training and ran navigational missions. Oddly there were even night flights where navigators had to use celestial navigation. It was odd, because at the time of our training, the B-17 bombing runs out of England were all in the daytime, and night bombing was in the hands of the British.

If we didn't have celestial navigation training I would not have had a night training flight, with our newly arrived navigator, to think about. We took off from our Tennessee air base after dark on a beautiful starry night, and the plan was to fly straight north for an hour or so, then west, then southeast to our original north vector, and then south to our base. It initially appeared to be a simple mission, assuming of course that Chuck knew how to read the stars and manipulate his sextant. He undoubtedly had been reasonably well trained, for after several hours of zigzagging he finally had us on the home course heading right for our base. Dick and I were not too concerned until we noticed Chuck standing in the dark behind our seats. When we turned around to look at him he asked, "Why didn't you land?" He had brought us back over the "blacked-out" air base (or close enough), and had meticulously closed up his books and maps, and had been watching us fly merrily along for quite some time. He had just forgotten to tell us that we were back in our landing zone and that it was time to land. After a bit of radio directional work we determined that we were well on our way toward the Gulf of Mexico. It was no major problem to get back to the base, but I learned on that mission that I had better, in the future, keep an eye on everything that goes on. Even though overshooting the airfield was rather funny, it was still my plane and my responsibility.

I had one other reminder of my responsibility as the pilot and commander of my crew. We had been on a gunnery training flight, shooting at ground and air targets, and generally having a good time. When we were through and heading back to our base it was time to clear our guns and get ready for landing. The procedure for the ball turret gunner was to climb out of the turret after pointing the guns straight down which positioned the turret hatch up and into the floor of the fuselage. After the gunner climbed out, the guns had to be repositioned

17

to point toward the rear of the ship, ninety degrees from the down position. My gunner forgot to do the repositioning and answered positively when Dick, using the intercom, checked to see if everyone was ready to land. I then brought the ship down for a pretty good landing and felt that we had completed another successful training mission. However, when it was time for us to move on to our next assignment I discovered I could not clear the base until I settled up with the Finance Department. It seemed I was charged, and had to reimburse the Army, for two machine gun barrels that somehow interfered with the runway and got ground off when I landed the plane. I can't remember the exact cost, but it was about ninety dollars, reminding me again of the price of command.

Another night navigational mission impressed on me the value of Staff Sergeant Harold S. Derr, "Pappy" to the crew. Pappy had been in the Air Corps longer than the rest of us and had earned his stripes as a ground crew radio operator and instructor. He was more than qualified to take over the radio communications on our B-17.

He was also quite adept at taking and sending Morse code.

The night mission was an exercise to give Chuck more "dead reckoning" experience. "Dead reckoning" is simple navigation. The plane is just flown from point to point by compass direction and elapsed time, with some correction for wind direction and velocity. Simple— when all goes well and ground lights can be seen. On this particular flight nothing seemed to go well and cloud cover prevented Chuck from verifying ground checkpoints. Chuck had to assume we were on course. At 2:00 in the morning we were supposedly heading right towards our base that as usual was blacked out except for the rotating beacon light. We saw the light through the overcast and dropped down to buzz the tower to request runway lights and landing instructions. When we got low enough to see the ground—there was no tower. We were not over our base. A little wooden building and what looked like a single concrete runway were below us. Certainly not our air base!

We buzzed the building several times, until a man

came out and stared up at our plane. We undoubtedly got him out of bed. We could not make radio contact; and we had to know where we were as our fuel supply was not overly abundant. Pappy, however, had the solution. He got out our "biscuit gun" (a light gun that is used to transmit Morse code), and did some signaling. The man got the idea and went back into the building and returned with his light gun and started flashing code at us. With all the hours Dick and I had spent learning to take and receive code, via key and radio, interpreting light flashes was way out of our league. But not for Pappy. Over the intercom he told us he had learned the name of the field and its location relative to a nearby town. We had no trouble locating our position on our map, and I wiggled our wings to thank our ground helper and flew a compass heading back to our base. We were about twenty minutes away. I sure was glad we had a guy like Pappy on board to support the rest of us. I also learned when on these navigational missions to always keep a radio-compass check on our position.

From operational training, we went by train to a staging

area outside New York City. The train trip as usual for wartime was long and slow, but eventually we arrived at Fort Dix, New Jersey for staging, which is the final preparation for transfer to overseas duty. For hours on end, over the next few days, we had the latest directives, commonly referred to as "poop," drilled into us. There was a good bit of information on escape and evasion tactics, and how we were expected to handle ourselves if we were unlucky and were captured and interrogated by the enemy.

We then traveled at amazing speed (for the military) through long lines from window to window, where we received some new equipment, including for aircrews the issue of a .45-caliber automatic and a matching shoulder holster. Then from desk to desk to complete the paperwork to clear our biggest base—The United States of America. In no time at all, we found ourselves en route to our Hudson River port of embarkation and "alerted" for shipment.

As a rule, about half of the bomber crews sent to England fly new ships over the Atlantic. This is a flight to thrill the heart of any airman. But, we, being in the other half, had to be content and somewhat less thrilled with just going on a long ocean voyage on one of the largest and must luxurious ocean liners, the *Queen Mary*. I was excited by the prospect of the trip, having never in all my life crossed any body of water larger than an inland lake. We left the port after dark and, as the *Queen Mary* was a fast ship and could outrun German submarines, we sailed alone without a convoy.

When we climbed up the gangplank, we had to return our newly acquired automatics. Disappointing, but I guess they were recycled to the next batch of aircrews on their way to the ETO.

As officers, Bill, Chuck, Dick and I shared a first class stateroom with bath. The ship was British and as the British Army and Navy were very rank conscious, our crew was billeted below decks in crowded quarters for enlisted personnel. The USO people on board, regardless of several with well-known Hollywood names, were also relegated to the lower decks. To enable the ship to reach maximum speed the stabilizing gyroscopes had been removed and the rolling of the ship made most everyone sick, especially the poor guys in the crowded below-deck quarters. We kept our crew "top-side" with us, as much as possible, sharing the most important feature of our cabin, the shower.

In three and a half days, after an uneventful crossing, we landed in Scotland and were officially attached to the Eighth Air Force. We had arrived as replacements, and as replacements we were classified by crews and sent to the operational bomb groups needing us. Our assignment to the 447th Bomb Group was made at an orientation center at the Scottish port, and after a train and bus ride we found ourselves at an air base in Suffolk, England and part of a real operational fighting force. We were ready and eager to begin the job that we had been trained to do.

CHAPTER 3

MISSION TO MERSEBURG

DECEMBER 6, 1944 WAS FOR ME REALLY A memorable date. It was a date that ended my active combat days with the United States Army Air Corps, and a date that started me down the road of this present adventure. At 0330 (Army time), I was roused from my slumber by the squadron CQ and told I was scheduled to fly a combat mission that morning. The briefing was set at 0430, breakfast in the next half hour, and topped off "Tokyos" was the order of the day. Topped off "Tokyos" meant the planes would have the fuel tanks in the outer wing panels completely filled for a long haul. This left little doubt in my mind, and in the minds of my co-pilot and navigator when I awakened them, as to our target. The Eighth Air Force had been pounding Merseburg, Germany, a synthetic oil refinery, day after day, and it was a long haul. A trip that used up every drop of gas that the ships could carry—a trip that required topped off "Tokyos."

As the three of us (Dick, Chuck, and myself) hurried to breakfast through the English mist, we were just a little bit squeamish about the probable target. Up to now our half dozen missions were either training or were what they call "milk runs," targets with little or no German resistance. Merseburg, if that's where we were going, was not a "milk run", it was one of the roughest targets in all of Germany. A target defended by hundreds of anti-aircraft guns and gunners, and the concentrated flak that they put in the sky had taken a significant toll of men and ships.

Down by the mess hall, we met the rest of our crew coming from their breakfast. I had never seen them in better spirits, and as we paused for a short greeting, I was assured that they were ready to take on any target in

Germany. They left us to attend their gunners' briefing, and we hurried to breakfast before our own briefing.

The briefing room was humming with activity, and it wasn't long after we arrived that the doors were closed and locked and the briefing began. Breaths were held and hearts pounded as the curtain was pulled from the map and our flight to the target was disclosed to us in red ribbon. The target? Merseburg. We had guessed it, and the confirmation made my pulse beat faster.

When the formation sheets were passed out, I was amazed and puzzled at our assigned position. I was to fly right wing of the lead ship in our squadron—the deputy lead position. It was one of the most important positions in the squadron formation, and with our limited experience I felt something was wrong. However, if that was where our group command wanted me to fly, I was ready and eager to get started.

The briefing continued and we were presented with all kinds of information: expected fighter cover, formations, radio frequencies, flare colors, all the many things we had to know were thrown at us in rapid succession.

Flare colors are particularly important. Hundreds of planes, from all over England that generally participate in a bombing mission, break through the overcast and into the dark morning sky at about the same time. A specific colored flare fired from a lead ship is the only guide a pilot has to get his plane in its proper flight position. The flares make organization out of chaos. Then the Colonel with his final orders ended the briefing, and we rushed to our lockers to get into our flying clothes.

It wasn't much later when I received the first bit of the bad luck I was soon to experience. Chuck Olson, my navigator, was attending his special briefing, and my co-pilot, Dick Fuller, and I were waiting outside for a truck to take us to our ship when we saw our squadron CO approaching. I was sure he wasn't bringing good news when I saw a new formation sheet in his hand. I was right. The formation had been changed, and because I had only an enlisted man for bombardier, I was moved from the deputy lead position to a spare position in the squadron. Bill, my bombardier, had been whisked away a few days before for special training and one of the crew, the armorer/gunner, had been selected to take his place temporarily. The new position was anything but good, but it did offer a possibility of filling any aborted position that might later occur. The Major wished us good luck and Dick and I piled into a waiting truck, and were taken to the "hard-stand," where our plane was parked.

Blanco Diablo was the ship we were to fly that day— "White Devil" when translated from the Spanish. What an airplane it was! Smooth and easy on the controls, and with a combat record hard to equal. A late model B-17G that couldn't be in better condition. It should be in good condition, for *Blanco Diablo*'s ground crew chief was Christy Ortolani, a good friend from high school. We had graduated together five years before, and I was incredibly surprised to run into him on the base shortly after we had arrived. I was extremely pleased that *Blanco Diablo* was Christy's baby to keep in tip-top shape.

When we reached the ship, the rest of the boys were already there and were busy installing their guns and helping the crew chief. The wings of the ship were white with frost, and members of the ground crew were using liquid de-icer and plenty of elbow grease to remove it. Dick climbed into the ship and "went on radio" while my engineer and I began our usual pre flight check. Turbo wheels okay, tires and struts filled, gas, oil, ailerons, flaps, antennas, everything ready and waiting to go. Personnel equipment was checked, oxygen masks, flak suits, helmets, "Mae Wests" (our personal flotation vests), all were on board and okay.

Soon Chuck arrived by truck, completing the crew, and we all took our positions in the ship to await the starting time. As I passed through the bomb bay on my way to the cockpit I remember patting one of the dark gray five-hundred-pound bombs that had been loaded in the racks. Soon they would be dropped straight into Der Fuhrer's lap.

The B-17 heavy bomber crews flying in the ETO varied slightly in the number of men in the crew. The position of the ship in the formation determined the size of its crew, and visa versa. My crew on this mission consisted of six enlisted men and three officers and our function, as most others, was to fly a wing position.

In recounting my "adventure" I have mentioned my co-pilot, Dick Fuller, and Chuck Olson, my navigator. We were the three officers. Five Corporals and one Staff Sergeant made up the rest of the crew. Harold S. Derr, the Staff Sergeant, was my radio operator. My engineer was Don Holmes, my temporary bombardier was Joe Marlowe, and my gunners were Lowell Strain, Hank Rutkowski, and Loel Bishop. Almost as soon as we were "crewed up," way back in Lincoln, Nebraska, Harold Derr, the oldest at twenty-six, was dubbed "Pappy" and Bishop became just "Bish." Pappy and his boys were inseparable, and seemed more like brothers than just members of the same combat crew.

Don Holmes stood behind Dick and me as we started the engines that morning. His eyes were glued to the instrument panel, double-checking our every act. Chuck was in the nose, beginning his work on the flight log, Pappy was on radio, and Bish was in the tail gunner's position standing by with a light-gun to warn off other ships in the morning darkness.

Orders clicked in my earphones and soon after taxiing

to the runway in a line of roaring B-17s, I was opening my throttles and racing down the runway. We were off! The wheels were up! Turbos off, and the power reduced to forty-six inches at 2500 rpm. Things come fast on take-off, but there's no greater thrill in all flying than that race into the air.

The formation was assembling above the usual over-cast at 15,000 feet in semi-darkness. Our group lead was firing green-green flares, and shortly after we had climbed to assembly altitude, we were assembled and in position. The group then swung into its position in the bomber column and we began to climb on course to Germany.

It was an icy cold morning and the temperature was dropping steadily as we climbed upward. When we finally leveled off at 27,000 feet, our outer garments were white with frost, and the temperature was 48 degrees below zero. Thousands of feet below us, as we plowed on our way, a big deck of stratus clouds hid our progress. The clouds hid from all on the ground the white foam of our vapor trails. Faintly distinguishable to us were the fast moving silhouettes of our little friends, our fighter escort in their P-51 Mustangs. We could see them above and below and far out on the horizon. As a "Limey" would say, "It was a good show."

Our position in the formation was anything but satisfactory, and I began to look for a vacant position for us to fill. Dick, from his seat, was able to see the squadrons flying above and to our left. He saw the number six position in the low element vacated, and we didn't waste any time wheeling ourselves into the empty spot. This new position was the "low-low" spot in the formation and was vulnerable to fighter attacks, but it was an improvement on our previous "spare" position. Little did we know that we would soon discover just how bad a change we had made.

Coast in! Soon we would be over enemy territory. Our formation began to tighten, and I could see shell cases dropping from the other ships as the gunners test fired their guns. The radio was silent except for quick decisive messages between the group "leads." Over the intercom at five-minute intervals, Chuck would take oxygen checks and the snappy answers would come back, "Tail okay, Waist, okay, Ball, okay," and so on throughout the ship.

We had entered the continent by way of the Zuider Zee, crossing over occupied Holland. Before long Chuck gave me a position report putting us well over Hitler's fortress—Germany. After what seemed an endless time of close-formation flying, the IP, initial point, was approaching. We began to prepare ourselves for the coming trip from the IP, down the bomb run to Merseburg. We helped each other into our flak jackets and put on our steel helmets. Don drained the hydraulic system to keep the high-pressure tank in the cockpit from exploding if hit by shell fragments. We were ready, and I glanced at the clock to check the remaining time.

We were not all ready, however, for it seemed that one of the crew had inadvertently used someone's helmet as a portable "john." Obviously that someone was a bit annoyed and our intercom was busy, for a minute or so, to get either the mess cleaned up or straightened out. The incident helped relieve the obvious tensions of the moment.

At the IP, the three squadrons in our group broke formation and made the turn onto the bomb run in "trail," and then, as part of our squadron, we headed straight in to our target. Tension was high. Last minute orders came over the radio, and in the ship the crew searched the sky for German fighters.

Black puffs of flak would be marking our target, and I kept looking ahead of my lead ship to where it would soon appear. Then, God, there it was! Not puffs, but almost a solid black cloud. A solid cloud of the dreaded flak. The ships ahead entering the flak area disappeared, almost completely, as the black mass closed around them. I had heard from others a good deal about the Merseburg flak barrages. They were heavy barrages, always deadly, and now for the first time I was about to witness one first hand. Soon, we would be in the midst of that seemingly solid black cloud.

Our bomb bay doors were now open. In the lead ships

the bombardiers were peering through their sights, and the time dragged on as we slowly closed on the target. Now the hundreds of black puffs from exploding shells that made up that black cloud were getting awfully close. I watched and saw the first shell explode within our formation and knew we were in it at last. The puffs came fast now—all around us. So near we could hear the dull sound of the explosions above the drone of our engines.

Would they never drop those bombs? Hurry! My God, those shells were near. Then, at last, bombs were away, and the ship expressed my relief as it zoomed upward 6,000 pounds lighter. As Dick reached forward to trigger the switch to close the bomb bay doors, the ship shuddered violently. We were hit, but I had no time to think of damage, as my "lead" was turning into me. I racked the ship hard to stay with him, but experienced a sinking feeling as I felt trouble in the controls. The flak was coming closer again. Red flashes could be seen as the shells burst. Again, the plane shuddered as a ripping, tearing sound pierced my ears! We were hit, and hit bad! I looked wildly around for signs of damage, hoping against hope it wasn't bad. But there it was—a gaping hole through the wing. The wing—the most important part of the airplane—the part that kept us in the air—was badly damaged. The ship acted strangely, and I struggled to keep it under control. My tail gunner was yelling over the intercom that part of our tail was also gone but that he was okay. The formation was passing overhead, and I dove to gain speed.

I was fighting the controls and from the heavy "yaw" I knew we had lost an engine. To take the pressure off the controls I needed "trim," and I kicked the trim in with my foot. At the same time I bent the throttles forward for more speed to get out of the area. The flak was still around us but less intense. Thank God, we were almost out of immediate danger. The formation was above and ahead, but I was confident that we would catch up with it shortly.

Dick had checked the crew by intercom. They were all okay. He had ordered the ball turret gunner out of his position, as the ball was now flooded with gasoline. The hole in the wing had split one of our fuel tanks wide open and the gas had poured out and back over the plane. The fuel pressure gauge showed number four engine to be without fuel. The engine gauge showed it had no power. I gave Dick the controls and feathered the windmilling prop. One engine out. That wasn't too bad. She would fly on three. I poured on the coal to catch the formation.

To keep up with the formation with only three engines would require lots of power, and to catch up with the others, every bit of horsepower those three engines could produce had to be used. I increased power and rpm till the engines whined in protest, but the distance between us and the other ships began to close and shortly we were again nestled in our position. I relaxed on the power and had just began to feel a bit more secure, when heavy clouds of black smoke began to pour from number one engine. It was on fire! The smoke's color told me it was burning oil, and the perspiration ran down my face as I realized how close we were to disaster.

As before, I went through the frequently practiced feathering procedure, but this time I raced the engine as the propeller began to feather, hoping to blow out the fire. It worked. The old SOP (Standard Operating Procedure) worked, and a surge of relief went through me as the smoke cleared and finally ceased altogether.

Again, we were behind the formation. I couldn't keep up with only the two inboard engines, and the ship wasn't even holding altitude. The ship was in a glide and all the power I could get from the remaining two engines wouldn't hold us up. Something had to be done. German fighters were around and if they attacked us, by ourselves, out of formation, they would shoot us to pieces. We had to get back in formation. Number one engine looked all right. Perhaps the fire was only caused by some small flak damage. Now that the fire was out it might stay out—even if the engine were running. It was worth a try. So I attempted to restart number one. It turned over and seemed to run okay, but a check of the gauges showed that the engine was providing a bare eight inches of manifold pressure, which was a measure of power. The engine wasn't even pulling enough to counteract its own drag. So, again, it was feathered. . . .

I knew then that old *Blanco Diablo* would have to go

home by itself. The prospect of that lonely trip looked pretty grim. We were losing altitude fast. I could see the bomber column above pulling away from us. We were alone. Alone over the area where most of the Luftwaffe's fighters were to be found. Dick, over the UHF (Ultra High Frequency) radio tried, and succeeded, in making contact with our group lead. He gave our position and asked for fighter cover. On the intercom I told the crew to start throwing everything not nailed down out of the ship. The altimeter needle kept going slowly around and all the power we could get from our two engines wouldn't keep us up. The gaping hole we had in the wing was undoubtedly reducing our lift. The ship was almost at the stalling speed. We were indicating between 100 and 105 miles per hour. Looking back through the ship, I could see the crazy, nose high attitude we were holding.

It wasn't five minutes after Dick's urgent message to the group lead, that one of the crew called, "Fighters!" I held my breath and waited, but the familiar silhouette of a P-51 loomed up and not the dreaded German Messerschmitt, the Me.109. There they were, all around us, our

P-51's. Beautiful and shiny—our escort—looking like silver angels to me.

The crew was working like mad throwing guns, ammo, extra flying clothes, tools, radio parts, anything they could get their hands on overboard. I could feel the effect as the lightened ship became less mushy and I could see the altimeter needle slow down its ceaseless turning. I used the intercom again and ordered the ball turret jettisoned. That would have to do, as there was nothing else to throw overboard. Then, when the ball dropped away from the ship, twisting and turning as it fell toward the ground—thank God!—we began to hold our own. Fifteen thousand feet! We could hold it. After losing thirteen thousand feet, we were now light enough to hold a constant altitude. True, we were still at stalling speed and at a dangerous altitude, but we were safe for the moment.

All the time we were fighting to maintain altitude I had been holding the ship on the path of the bomber column. Now, we had to pick a new course. We had barely enough gas in our remaining tanks to make the coast, and perhaps Brussels. But between us and any friendly airfield was a wall of flak. In some places this wall was thick and virtually impossible to cross. In other places, where the flak guns were farther apart, our ship could possibly slip through. Places like these are termed "flak channels," and were displayed on Chuck's map. I set up the auto-pilot and turned the ship over to the gyros. Chuck came up from the nose, and the three of us, Dick, Chuck and I, went into a huddle to pick the best route to follow to safety. Oxygen masks were thrown aside, as at fifteen thousand feet, we were below the altitude where we needed

constant oxygen.

We decided, after looking at the map, to change our course slightly to the south and continue on into Holland. We would then make a left turn, pass through a flak channel, and on into friendly territory. It looked easy—perhaps too easy, but for the first time since losing the second engine we all felt, inside, that we would make it back. "Fate," miserable "Fate," seemingly had other plans.

Just as we approached the Holland border, number two engine began to throw oil. I watched the steady oozing of the black blood from under the cowling for as long as I could. I closed the cowl flaps to hide the sight. The end was coming now. Soon number two would be dry and would freeze up. The ship, in its damaged condition, would not fly on just one engine. The oil pressure gauge began to flicker and started to show a decline in pressure; and the oil temperature gauge began to climb as the insufficient amount of oil began to heat. The standard procedure in the event of an oil failure is to feather the prop and shut off the engine before the pressure dropped to forty pounds. I knew this as I watched the pressure drop off. But I also knew that I could not keep flying on only one engine. I made the decision, as the needle showed forty pounds, to skip the feathering and to run the engine bone dry. I could possibly get another five minutes of operation before it would freeze. Dick, looking over at me, winked as he reached under his seat for his parachute. He knew my next move would be to flip the switch, sounding the alarm bell, to prepare the crew to abandon ship. Dick warned the crew over the intercom and gave them our position over Holland. I would have liked to have the radioman contact our base to inform them we were going down, but unfortunately we had jettisoned most of the radio equipment to lighten the ship. The P-51 escort was still keeping tabs on us and I was sure they would relay the bad news. With nothing else to do, I twisted in my seat and fastened my black English "escape" shoes to my harness and hooked on my chute. The escape shoes, not new, not old, were certainly better suited to evading capture then the tell-tale heavy flying boots we were wearing in the ship.

When the altitude was around eight thousand feet, number two quit and pieces from the engine began to break off and fly back over the wing. The time had come. I tripped the alarm bell, ordering the crew to jump, and Dick and I climbed out of our seats.

I glanced back through the ship, waved good-bye to the boys, and leaned forward to pat Joe on the back as he was about to leave through the navigator's hatch. I didn't see Chuck, so I figured he was already out. The ship was now empty except for Dick and me. Dick flipped the switch opening the bomb bay doors and we went back together to go out through the bomb bay. The altimeter had indicated four thousand feet. After shaking hands, we left the ship.

I had often thought about making a parachute jump and wondered how I would feel before throwing myself out into open space. My only recollection now is that I jumped from the bomb bay with little concern. I can't recall giving much thought to the height or the danger involved. I had to go, and I was more anxious to get out of the falling ship than I was to stay in.

CHAPTER 4

HOLLAND

I POPPED MY CHUTE SHORTLY AFTER LEAVING the ship, and my heart really did pound as I waited the few seconds before the white silk began to stream from the pack. I was mighty relieved when the canopy fully opened and I felt the jerk halting my downward plunge. The silence was deafening and I spoke aloud to reassure myself of my hearing. Glancing around I saw my ship heading toward the earth and I guess I said, "Good-bye." In the other direction, I counted six parachutes floating through space. I wondered if the other two were already on the ground.

Looking down, I was brought back to reality with a

start. I was drifting over a road on which a mob of people was gathered. They were pointing or waving at me, and I could barely hear the sound of their voices. From my height, and to my relief, I was unable to distinguish any German soldiers. I drifted beyond the road toward long stretches of flooded fields. Almost without warning I hit the ground. The last few feet had been hard to judge, but I hit easy, up to my knees in water. I had no trouble collapsing my chute and, sloshing around through the water, I rolled the chute into a bundle.

To escape and hide was my only thought. I began to run through the cold water away from the road and the people I had seen. I reached the field's edge, and threw my chute in the bushes, covering it as best I could with dead leaves and brush. I was winded, but I dared not pause to rest. I started across the next field toward what seemed to be higher and rougher country. I don't know how many fields I crossed, but even though the higher fields were not flooded, between each were ditches, waist deep, filled with muddy water, barbed wire, and brush. My clothes were torn and I was soaking wet from my waist down. My legs were numb as I forced them to carry me farther and farther. My boots were filled with the ice-cold water, and they squished and squashed with my every step.

In the next field, a man was standing watching me. He looked to be a farmer, and he waved as I approached. I needed help and I must try to obtain it from someone. The man smiled and held out his hand as I came close to him, and I shook it with relief. I pointed at myself and almost shouted, "American, American. Can you help me?" The farmer only shook his head and pointed at his ears. From behind, an old man was approaching. The farmer pointed at him, and said, "My father." Or something sounding like father. The old man held out his hand to me and I shook it gladly, but I couldn't make him understand I wanted help and that I wanted to be hidden from the Germans. The word "German" made him pound his chest and say, "Hollander. Hollander." That was all I could get out of him. I was wasting my time, so I took off again, stumbling across the muddy land, fighting for every breath. The stabbing pain in my side that got worse with every step, and the reddish haze that colored my vision from my pounding blood, told me I had to stop. I don't know how, but I managed to get to the next clump of bushes. I gave in to my exhaustion and threw myself in their midst. The bushes were on the edge of a ditch and I was half in and half out of the chilling water, but too tired to care, I lay gasping for air and prayed to God to not let me be caught.

The cold was terrific and I began to shiver as it seeped through my wet clothing. My flying clothes were heavily insulated but when soaked with water they were of little use. I noticed then that I was still wearing my bright yellow "Mae West." I tore it off and pushed it deep into the bushes. I cursed myself for my neglect in forgetting to remove the telltale garment. I hoped it had not caused me to be seen by the Germans. Just in case, I forced myself to my feet and ran across another field putting just a little more distance between me and the people who saw me land. A little more distance toward safety.

Again I crouched in a hedgerow of naked bushes to rest, and it was from this questionable refuge I saw a small group of figures running in my direction. I couldn't quite make them out. My breathing was in short gasps as I burrowed myself deeper into the bushes. With my strength all but gone I lay there and watched like some hunted animal.

Despite the cutting cold, I could feel the perspiration break out on my forehead as I watched the band of men skirt the edge of the adjacent field. They must have seen me as their path led invariably towards my scant refuge. Scarcely breathing, I watched their approach, puzzled somewhat about the way they walked and ran. They weren't soldiers. There were no uniforms among them. They were civilians and seemed to be hardly more than boys. Should I show myself to them? Perhaps they would supply me with the help I needed so badly. Then again, maybe they were only curious kids, and no good could come from being made the center of attention. Still, they were Dutch, and the Dutch were our allies. Then with sudden decision, I rose from my refuge and pushed my way out of the bushes. The boys seeing me waved, but refrained from any shouting, as they ran silently toward me. I raised my arm and waved back, and hoped to God I had done the right thing.

For the next few minutes, I was occupied shaking the hands of six smiling boys. They were not children, despite their somewhat childlike dress. They appeared to be boys in their mid teens. Here was the help I needed. In spite of my exhaustion and concern, I smiled in relief. One of the boys spoke a little English and asked in slow halting words, "Are—you—wounded?" I answered that I was not. And the boy continued, "Come—with—us—quickly. We—will—help—you." He then pointed in the direction from which they had come and said, "soldiers—Germans." My fatigue was forgotten as I ran with the boys along the edge of the field toward a narrow dirt path. The group followed the path a short way toward higher, drier ground, and here they stopped. The boys motioned for me to lie down in a dry ditch at the edge of the path. Sinking down gladly I watched and wondered what was to happen next as I saw one of the younger boys go trotting off alone down the path. Well, I was in their hands now, and in spite of the danger surrounding me in a land filled with enemies, I felt immensely relieved.

It was not long after the boy disappeared around the bend in the path when he reappeared, jogging beside a bicycle ridden by a youngish woman. She wore a long black coat and black knee boots. In contrast, a gaily colored scarf covered her head. Behind her, seated sideways on the luggage carrier of the bicycle, was another woman. She was similarly dressed and quite similar in features to the other. I judged them to be sisters. Probably in their late twenties or early thirties. I stayed where I was, lying in the ditch, and watched as the boys moved down the path to meet them. The first woman talked to the boys, gesturing with her hands and pointing in the way from which we had come. I wished I could understand them. I was feeling my helplessness rather acutely. I knew I was in for rough times ahead, but now my future seemed to be in the hands of others and somewhat out of my control.

The woman, reaching into a bag tied to the crossbar of

the bicycle, pulled out a small bundle of clothes and handed it to one of the boys. The English-speaking lad came over to me and said, "You—must—change—clothes—now. You—must—look—like—us." Now things were beginning to happen, and I reached gladly for the bundle of clothes. Speed must have been essential, for the boys with many hands helped me to get out of my outer flying jacket, to pull off my insulated boots and pants and finally my electric flying suit, which without batteries was obviously useless. My shirt was not very wet and I was told to keep it on. But my tie was removed and a boy gestured to my collar, which I rolled under. The main item of clothing the women had brought was a pair of ragged blue coveralls. I climbed into these, and put on my "escape" shoes. The coveralls buttoned right up to the neck so my shirt did not show. I was glad I still had it on for its extra warmth. One of the boys looped a long gray scarf around my neck. He left the ends long and hanging down my back. This was the way the other boys were wearing their scarves. They placed a gray beret on my head, covering my hair completely. My costume was complete, and the boys stood back to look me over. The women laughed and one said, "You—Holland—boy." The English-speaking boy added, "Now you—look—like—us." They then picked up my discarded clothes, and from my pants, transferred my only possessions to the pockets of my coveralls: a handkerchief, a comb, and my Army identification card. I had kept my dog tags that were on a chain around my neck. The boys wanted to see the card, and they tried pronouncing my name. Lieutenant, sounded like the British Leftenant, my first name, Howard, was too difficult for them, but my own Dutch last name, "DeMallie," came easy. "You—officer?" I nodded. "Officer," the word was murmured through the group. "What the heck," I thought, I'm only a Second Lieutenant, but from the way they were looking at me they must have thought a Lieutenant was someone pretty important.

One of the women began to speak rapidly, pointing again down the path. The boys nodded in agreement.

"We—go—now," the boy told me, then also pointing back from where we had come, he said, "Germans." The women waved and took off on their bicycle, and the group of us started across the fields, breaking away from the path. We no longer ran, but walked along at a normal rate. I was able to straighten up and look freely over the countryside for the first time. One of the boys pointed at my watch that was visible below the sleeve of my coveralls. I slipped it off and put it in my shirt pocket. My interpreter said, "American—watch. Don't—wear." My vocabulary was increasing, and I received approving smiles when I said, "Ya." Another boy motioned for me to put my hands in my pockets, and I suddenly realized that I was walking along swinging my arms while they, all of them, sort of shuffled along with their hands in their pockets. I tried to match their shuffle and felt that I was doing it fairly well.

We were coming to a small woods and as we entered its marshy darkness, one of the boys, who was carrying my clothes, branched off by himself. Undoubtedly, he was going to hide or bury them someplace. Stopping in a small clearing, we all sank to the ground and the boys' actions led me to believe that we were going to stay for a while. I was right, for the English-speaking lad said in his halting manner, "We—stay—here—till—dark." Then, in response to a question from one of the others, he asked, "Where—parachute?" I told him as best I could where I had hidden it. Relaying my message to the others, my interpreter said, "We—will—try—and—find— to—bury." Two of the boys then left, and retraced our path. There were four boys left as the lad who had disposed of my clothes had rejoined us. The oldest appearing boy of the group sat down on the grass next to me and pulled a can of tobacco from his pocket and handed it to me with a cigarette paper. "Smoke?" he asked. What an idea. I didn't realize how badly I wanted a cigarette until that moment. Nodding my head to indicate a definite yes, I tried to roll my first hand-made cigarette. Life in the USA had not trained me to roll my own, and I was making a mess of what looked like a simple rolling procedure. The boy, laughing, took the paper from my hands and with dexterity and skill, rolled the cigarette, motioning me to lick the edge myself. I did so, and stuck down the edge. The boy rolled one for himself and striking a match, lit us up. The other boys were similarly occupied.

The English-speaking boy was slightly built and had longish dark hair. He came over and squatted at my side, and I could see him forming the words he meant to use with his lips, and then, "You—gunner?" "No," I answered, "I was the pilot." "Pilot," the boy murmured. "You—fly—the—plane?" And he emphasized the question with a pointing finger. "Yes," I said. I had to smile at the incredulous look on his face. If he could only see the hundreds of thousands of Uncle Sam's Fly Boys, he wouldn't be so amazed.

Officer and pilot. He couldn't seem to get over that. I watched as he formed his next words, and then he asked, "How—many—with—you?" "Oh, oh," I thought. Be careful, DeMallie. Outside of my struggle across the fields, this evasion has been pretty easy up to now. Maybe it's a trick. I smiled at him to show my lack of animosity, and said, "I can't tell you that." "Oh," he said, and smiled himself. "All right, but," his eyes took on a peculiar look and he now no longer smiled. "One—with—you," he continued, "is—dead." The words took a moment to register with me. My stomach felt strange and light. "Dead," I murmured. And for the moment, I couldn't quite grasp the thought. I don't believe I showed the slightest change of expression. We were all so alive a little while ago. "Who was it?" I finally asked. The boy shook his head and said, "I—do—not—know." "Germans?" I asked. He shook his head again. "Parachute—still—closed—on—ground." A chill swept over me, and I could feel my eyes moisten. One of the boys had fallen straight to earth. I can't describe how I felt at the thought of that drop. I didn't know which of the boys it was, and I was afraid even to think of who it could be. The body must have been found nearby and I felt, rather than knowing for certain, that it was Dick, my co-pilot, as we had left the ship within seconds of each other. The Dutch boy expressed his sympathy by placing his hand on my shoulder. He made me understand through gestures and halting English that he had learned about the tragedy from the woman who brought my clothes.

CHAPTER 5

RESCUED BY
THE UNDERGROUND

I HAD LANDED ABOUT 2:30 IN THE AFTER-noon, and darkness began to close in about 4:00. I wondered a good deal about my next move, and really became concerned when the boys rose from the ground and began to say good-bye. The boy, who spoke for all, said they had to go home. I was afraid that soon I would be left to fend for myself. However, the boy, pointing to the oldest of the group, said I was to go with him to his home when it became much darker. I can say I was relieved. The boys filed off and I waved good-bye and thanked them in my heart.

Some time later the two of us were joined by a new boy, somewhat younger than the others. He spoke rapidly to the older boy, who I learned was his brother, and we started off through the woods. It was getting quite dark and was rather rough going. Soon, however, we left the woods and followed an old wagon road paralleling a small stream. The younger boy ran ahead and was swallowed up in the darkness. It must have been fifteen or twenty minutes later when we approached what seemed to be a collection of farm houses. We paused and my guide whistled softly into the darkness. Almost immediately, his whistle was answered and again we proceeded on our way. The number of houses increased and I could see we were entering a town. The wagon road branched off onto a brick road and we turned and walked down the paralleling sidewalk. Up ahead I could hear footsteps approaching. We quickly left the walk and waited in the deeper shadow of a large tree—friend or foe? The footsteps faded in the darkness . . .

After a few minutes whistles were again exchanged and we continued down the walk. Along the street, a cyclist passed us and my guide exchanged greetings with a wave. A whistle sounded again in the darkness, and my Dutch friend uttered, "Come." He took my arm and rushed me through a gate and down a walk leading to a house. The house was small with only one story and had a lean-to type barn attached to it. "My—house," my guide said, and he led me around the back and we entered the very dark barn. I stumbled behind him, passing a couple of barely discernible cow or horse stalls, to the back wall of the house.

The back door opened as we approached and the young boy was framed for an instant in candlelight. I entered and found myself in what seemed to be a parlor and kitchen combined. The only light came from a candle on the table and from a potbellied stove in the corner. Around the stove, the other occupants of the room were gathered. They seemed to be mostly children. They smiled at me as an old woman rose and shuffled toward me with outstretched hand. She led me to her chair and I sank into it, gratefully. The stove was warm, and I realized then how cold I actually was. I was shivering all over, and my wet feet were all but numb. The old woman poured me a cup of scalding tea. I sipped it slowly, enjoying its warmth dripping down my throat and burning my stomach. There was a lot of murmuring and talking among the family. I sat there trying to look composed, but felt too excited to even relax. I smiled at the kids and I focused my attention on the wooden shoes drying on top of the stove.

The actions of the people seemed to suggest to me that they were waiting for someone. I couldn't talk to any of them, and had to content myself with waiting and listening. I don't know how long I waited, but I relaxed and soon I found myself dozing off. The heat and tea had been too much for me, to say nothing of my recent experiences.

My eyes snapped open with a start, and I was wide awake when I heard a voice ask in English, "Is this the American flyer?" I looked around and saw a girl in a light tan raincoat standing behind me. I rose and answered somehow. I was too surprised to make an intelligent answer.

She smiled and said she was here to help me. I still couldn't believe it, for she was amazingly pretty with large dark eyes and long dark hair. It seemed more like a movie to me every minute. Then I noticed another woman waiting with her. She was one of the two women who had brought me clothes in the woods that afternoon. I greeted her, and then the girl with the dark hair said in rather good English, "Say good-bye to the others. You and I are going to go to another house." I shook the boy's hand and expressed my thanks as best I could to the two women and the rest of the household. The girl translated for me. Then, after the candles were blown out, we stepped out the side door and into the darkness.

As the door closed behind us, the girl reached out and took my arm. She led me out to the street and then diagonally across. We walked quickly down the far side and, before long we turned into the side yard of a large two-story brick house. My companion 'yoo-hooed' as we passed a protruding bay window, and the back door opened for us to enter. Inside I was very pleased to see that I was in the kitchen of a house somewhat similar to houses in America. Electric lights illuminated our path through the kitchen and across the hall and into the main room of the house. A dining table with chairs was in the center of the room and easy chairs, cabinets and a sofa were placed along the walls. The windows were heavily draped but everything inside was bright and cheerful, including the smiling faces turned toward me at my entrance.

A man of middle age rose from a chair by the round stove in the corner and approached to shake my hand. He introduced himself simply as Roelof. He welcomed me in halting English, and turned to place a chair for me by the stove. A middle-aged woman and a slim young girl, the other two members of the household, nodded to me, and the girl blushed deeply as the man laughingly said something to her. I soon found myself sitting in the chair by the fire with another cup of tea. I tried to keep up with what was going on, but there was entirely too much Dutch being spoken with only, occasionally, a question or two in English from the pretty dark-haired girl who had been my escort. I realized she had only a limited knowledge of English, and had to think a bit before she could speak.

Soon the girls began to set the table for supper. I was keenly aware of the hunger pains in my stomach. I had been afraid I had arrived too late for the evening meal, but now it appeared that my stomach had not been forgotten. Before supper was served, the dark-haired girl, who had introduced herself as "Mimi," led me upstairs to show me a change of clothes lying ready for me on the bed, and a place where I could wash up. For the first time in my life, I was glad to get into a pair of "long-johns." And, from that time on, I learned to swear by them.

When I had finished dressing in a pair of baggy dark blue pants, with a belt to hold them up, and a long sleeve cotton shirt with vertical stripes, I returned downstairs to find supper ready on the table. I certainly needed no coaxing to take my place at the table. The family bowed their heads in prayer, and then Roelof looking at me said what sounded like, "Eat Smartly." Mimi noticing my bewildered look, translated for me. "Eat Smartly" was really "Bon Appetit" in Dutch. (Later she even wrote it down for me, and for some reason I remember the spelling *Eet Smakelyk*). "Eat Smartly" I did, as I ate my first meal in Holland. The procedure was a bit strange to me at first, for the dark brown bread, the basis of the meal, was not to be held in the hand, but placed on the plate and consumed with a knife and fork. Cheese sliced on top and cold cuts completed the fare. But as a special guest, the woman of the house provided me two boiled eggs.

I was sitting again in my chair by the stove, the women cleaning the table, the man smoking his pipe. Everything seemed to be peaceful and ordinary, and I found it hard to believe that just outside German soldiers were going by. They were walking the streets, perhaps looking for me and the rest of my crew. It was hard to believe. Nothing seemed real anymore.

I returned to reality rather quickly, as the man rose from his chair, opened a drawer, and removed a black leather wallet. Mimi explained to me that Roelof was a policeman, and had been the first official to reach the body of my comrade. The wallet he was handing to me was my comrade's. He had taken it before any Germans arrived to claim the body. I held it in my hands and my hands began to tremble as I opened it slowly. Whose would it be? Which one of my boys didn't come through? The wallet was empty except for a few pieces of miscellaneous scrap paper that everyone seems to carry. All identification had been removed, just as we had been instructed to do before leaving on a mission. The only clue I found was a torn off part of a canceled bill, that had a telephone number written on the back. The printed side had as part of an address, Conway, South Carolina. Conway, South Carolina? I knew then that it belonged to Joe Marlowe, my substitute bombardier. Joe was from Conway. What a terrible crashing end for a nineteen-year-old kid. What a terrible end for anyone . . . that tumbling fall to the earth.

I gave Roelof back the wallet. He would take it in the morning to his headquarters to keep himself in the clear. Then I asked about the rest of the crew. Roelof didn't know much, just that some of the crew had already been captured by the Germans. He didn't know how many or who they were. He did know that some had landed in a town and had been taken prisoner immediately. I had to be satisfied for a while with that little information, but I hoped and prayed that some of the others had been as fortunate as I in avoiding capture.

I guess I must have been pretty tired out, for it wasn't much longer before I began to nod my head in sleep. Mimi, noting my effort to keep my eyes open, asked if I would like to go to bed. It hurt my pride to answer, "Yes," for it was still early, but I was completely worn out and exhausted. So I was escorted upstairs by one and all of the household. My room, it seemed, was to be in the garret. But before I was shown up the next narrow flight of stairs, Roelof stripped back the end of the hall carpet to reveal a trap door beneath. The door, when open, showed a small recess barely large enough to admit one person, but to assure them and to assure myself, I slid into the hole with ease. This was to be my hiding place if needed, and I sincerely hoped it would not be necessary for me to put it to use.

My bed in the attic was perfect. It was an old fashioned feather bed, and shortly after I sank into its midst, I was asleep. Mimi had told me I could sleep as late as I wanted to, and I fully intended to spend a long, long time in bed. My body ached, but the softness of the bed soothed my limbs and I slept, and slept, and slept.

CHAPTER 6

HIDING IN STAPHORST

THE SUN WAS SHINING BRIGHTLY THROUGH the attic window, when I again opened my eyes. My watch read ten o'clock. I had slept thirteen hours without once waking up, although in strange surroundings, I had no momentary wondering of where I was. Everything was clear to me the instant I awoke. For some time, I laid there piecing together, bit by bit, what had happened to me since the day before. Here I was in occupied Holland, safe for the moment from the Germans. I had by sheer luck escaped capture. Would I continue to be lucky and make my way back to friendly territory? It was not uncommon for flyers to "walk out" after being downed in enemy territory. Could I "walk out"? What had happened to the rest of my crew? Where were they?—Poor Joe. I knew where he was. Poor kid. Why did his chute fail to open? Why not mine? Or one of the others'?

I went over, in my mind, piece by piece, the struggle that we had with our damaged ship. I wondered then, as I often wonder to this day, if I did everything possible to get that ship back. Even now, reflecting back, I'm quite sure I did, but that morning in that attic, I could only pray that I had.

My thought process came to an abrupt end as I heard footsteps on the attic stairs. The door opened quietly, and upon seeing me awake a tall fair-haired young man with a big smile stepped into the room. "How goes it?" he asked in good American slang, and sitting on the side of my bed he held out his hand. "My name is Peter."

It was quite enjoyable to be able to talk to someone in English, and it was especially enjoyable to discover that this fellow was here to arrange my return to Allied hands.

I felt immensely relieved, for the job of getting back was no longer mine alone, but the job of an organization—the Dutch Resistance, of which Peter was a member.

My hopes never got a chance to soar too high, for Peter also told me that my chances of getting back within many months were mighty slim. There were times, he said, when it was no problem at all to smuggle men from Holland to Belgium to France and then over the mountains to Spain. From Spain the British would take over, and fly the men back to England. Since the "D-Day" invasion this escape route was no longer a reasonable choice, and lately, as the Rhine River was the dividing line between armies, it was virtually impossible. He assured me, however, that it was his job to try to get me back, and he would if at all possible. "At least," he then added in his Americanized English, "we will knock ourselves out to keep you from the damn Germans. At worst we may have to hide you close to the action and just wait for the Allies to take over the area."

Then I received some especially good news. Peter told me that I was not the only one of my crew to get away.

One other was in Dutch hands and now he, Peter, was going to see this other guy and if possible bring him back to join me. That was too good to be true. But then, all of this was too good to be true. Everything seemed to be going too smoothly.

Peter left me, and I washed and dressed. I visited the toilet, and made my way downstairs to where breakfast was ready and waiting. It was rather late and I had asked Peter to tell the folks not to bother with breakfast. He insisted that it was all right and no trouble at all. I was glad he insisted, because I was extremely hungry, and the breakfast was good. While I ate, Peter tuned in a small radio that he held in his lap to A.F.M., the Allied forces station. He used his body as an aerial, and when the volume got too loud, he would remove his fingers from the antenna post. I learned later that Peter loved big band swing music with a passion, and would listen to it whenever he could. Radios were forbidden in occupied Holland, and it would be bad for any Dutchman discovered owning or listening to a radio. Therefore, of necessity, Peter had to play his very softly.

73

There were many things Peter did that the Germans wouldn't like. For example, he and his Dutch Resistance buddies would "appropriate" guns, ammunition and food from the Germans. They also gathered weapons dropped in canisters from Allied planes, and distributed the guns and equipment to the many Resistance groups operating in the surrounding areas. Until the time when they could rise up in mass and fight along with Allied troops, the "Resistance" vented their hatred with continuing acts of sabotage against the Nazis. Although Peter was never specific, he would often disappear after curfew at night for what he would call a little fun. In this manner Peter and his friends carried on their own style of warfare. I don't know whether providing aid to Allied airmen, like me, was a sideline to their "other" activities, but I did learn that the lives of many good Dutch people had been lost in the process.

After I had finished breakfast, Peter said he would have to leave for the rest of the day, but would return in the evening. He said he couldn't promise, but he might be able to bring with him my other comrade who was in hiding not too far away. I couldn't hope enough that he would, and I wondered which one of the crew it would be. When Peter left, Mimi, who had stayed the night, brought me an English book and I sat in a chair away from the window to try and read. Mimi was Peter's fiancée, and a wonderful couple they made. Peter was tall and strongly built and very blond. Mimi, in contrast, had her long dark hair and eyes.

I had quite a time that day in Staphorst, Holland. (Staphorst being the name of the town.) I alternately spent my time downstairs with the family and hiding upstairs away from the prying eyes of callers. It seemed to me more chatty old women visited that day than there were people in the entire town. I could see them as they came up the walk toward the front door. Several were dressed in ankle length blue dresses that showed beneath their long dark embroidered coats, and wore white bonnets on their heads. All the visitors wore wooden shoes, which they left at the front door as they entered. When I asked why some were dressed in what I considered old style Dutch clothing, Mimi told me that Staphorst was a

religious village and most of the people dressed tradi-
tionally. Practically all the people in the rural areas,
during the sloppy winter days, wore wooden shoes.
Boots and rubbers were very hard to come by, especially
during the German occupation.

I had one frightening experience when I was almost
caught downstairs. I had just enough time to squeeze
beneath the sofa before another visitor entered through
the door. This time it was a German officer to see Roelof.
Roelof, I later learned, was not just a policeman, but the
Police Chief of the little town of Staphorst. The German
was calling on official business. Thankfully, not about
me. The German sat down on the sofa with me underneath, and I could see his boots just inches from my face.
I was in a cramped position and I dared not move,
breathe or, God forbid, sneeze. After what seemed like an
interminable time, the German finally got up and he and
Roelof left. How the women laughed when I finally came
out from under the sofa. I suspect their laughter was part
hysteria, but how could they laugh knowing that their
lives were in jeopardy had I been discovered. I admired

those Hollanders then, and now many decades later, my admiration for all the courageous Hollanders is enormous.

The day passed rapidly, and soon Roelof came home from work. He startled me no little bit as he burst in the door in his police uniform. I had never seen him in uniform before, and in my present situation, a uniform, to me, was something to be dreaded. Almost every uniformed figure could be my enemy.

After supper, the back doorbell rang and I hurried, as before, up the stairs to the second floor. These visitors weren't particularly dangerous to me, but it was best to keep out of sight. A stranger, in the house, would invite talk, and talk, no matter how harmless, might lead to my discovery and capture. And what would happen to these Dutch people sheltering me? They could only expect interrogation and death. A painful death for their efforts.

I was sitting quietly in the dark at the top of the stairs and I heard the back door open cautiously. I had been expecting Peter to come back, and now I could hear him speaking quietly to Mimi. Then I could hear footsteps pass through the back rooms below and on into the hall. Just to be on the safe side, I ducked back into a bedroom and closed the door to a crack. Footsteps on the stairs and labored breathing came to my ears. Then, illuminated by the glow of light from below, I could see the head and shoulders of Loel Bishop, my tail gunner, as he came into view. Bishop! Bishop was the one who had made it. Peter had brought him. God, I was happy to see him. I rushed to the stairs and on seeing me he called "Skipper, am I glad to see you!" He wasn't the only one glad to see someone, and I told him so. Seeing that he was hurt, I reached for his arm to help him up the last few steps.

Good old Bish. I couldn't believe it, but there he was with me in those unbelievable surroundings. He was dressed the way I was, but looked completely worn out. His right foot was wrapped in an old sweater and with his every movement he would wince with pain. He assured me his foot was all right, just badly sprained. He wiggled his toes to prove it was not broken, but the effort turned him pale. He sank with relief on the bed and asked me about the others. I couldn't tell him much, just the terrible news about Joe, and that some of the crew had been taken prisoner on landing. I was eager to have him tell his story, and he did as Peter began to bathe his foot.

Loel Bishop had been the first out of the ship, and had been down on the ground before I even opened my parachute. He landed on the edge of a town in a plowed field. When he hit there was a sharp pain in his foot and he was knocked unconscious. He opened his eyes a few minutes later to see he was in the center of a ring of curious people. He was too dazed to remember what he said or did, but a "whirlwind of efficiency" took charge of him. The "whirlwind" was a young Dutchman, who unbuckled his chute, rolled it up and handed it to one of the group. He then stripped him of his "Mae West" and flying clothes, giving them to the others. Helping Bish to his feet, he half carried him through the remaining streets and out of the town. Bish said he doesn't remember how long or how far they walked, but every step was misery, for his foot was crying in pain.

While I was sleeping in a feather bed, and I feel guilty just thinking about it, Bish was shivering in an old barn.

The young man who had helped him brought him some bread and sausage and left him there for the night. It was late the next afternoon before Peter arrived to take charge of him and to bring him to where I was staying. He had been alone for all that time and had almost given up hope of any assistance. He and Peter left the town after darkness had set in, and riding two on a bicycle, they made the trip to Staphorst.

Bish was the second youngest on my crew, being only nineteen years old. He was a tall, curly-haired kid, whose home was in Texas. Just before we had left the States, he had gotten married. His wife, Helen, had just turned eighteen. Somehow, seeing the mess he was in—we all were in—I felt responsible. It was foolish I guess to blame myself for the accuracy of the German flack, but all the pilots I have since talked to felt exactly the same way. The price, I guess, for being called "Skipper."

That night Bish and I shared the feather bed. I sank into its depths gladly and fell instantly asleep, but Bish's ankle was giving him so much pain that he was unable to sleep the whole night. The next day he bathed his ankle several times in vinegar and water, and Peter would bandage it tightly, hoping to reduce the swelling and the pain. Soon we would have to move on—and a sore ankle would present a difficult problem.

Our orders to move came sooner than any of us expected. In the afternoon a girl on a bicycle arrived and talked to Peter a few minutes and then left. Peter said that he had been given some information and we had to move that very evening. We were to be taken to a "safe" house in Meppel, a small city about eight kilometers away. Evidently there was some troop movement, and it was a now or never situation. Mimi and Peter were to go and stay with us, but I have to admit I felt a good deal of concern when I thought of that short but dangerous journey.

CHAPTER 7

JOURNEY TO MEPPEL

THE CURFEW TIME IN OCCUPIED HOLLAND, at the time of my unplanned visit, was 8:00 P.M., and the curfew was strictly enforced by the Germans. To take advantage of darkness, any movement we made had to be started after dusk, around 4:00 or 4:30, and had to be completed before curfew. Our trip to Meppel was planned to begin and end within those few hours.

Bish created a problem with his bad ankle, but he could be moved, as before, on the luggage carrier of a bicycle. He would be mighty conspicuous with his bandaged foot, but although it was dangerous it was also necessary, and chances had to be taken. The plans for the trip were simple, if not entirely foolproof. As near as I could gather five of us were to go. Bish, Peter, Mimi, Roelof's wife and I, all on bicycles. The two women were to ride ahead, both on one bike, and act as an advance guard. Peter and I were to follow some little distance behind. Bish would be riding with Peter. Two on a bike was not an uncommon sight in Holland as bicycles, like everything else, were in short supply.

At exactly the same time we were to leave the house, the girl, who had talked to Peter earlier, was to leave Meppel, and meet us about half way. She would be able to tell us whether the Germans were controlling the entrance to the city, and whether we could get through the road check. If everything was not all right, we would have to return to Staphorst and try another time.

I guess all of us were on edge the whole afternoon. I could not help but worry, for I knew this would be no picnic. However, the time passed rapidly, and soon, the winter darkness set in. We were to leave at five o'clock, and almost to the minute we shoved off. Quite a party— five of us on three bicycles. I said good-bye to Roelof, his wife, and daughter and thanked them again and again for all they had done for us. Roelof's wife was leaving with us, but I wouldn't be able to thank her again during the trip.

It was a perfect night for our ride—dark with a fine light rain. Early as it was, the darkness was so intense that the two women were swallowed up just a few yards down the road as they peddled out in front of us. Mimi carried a small lantern with a shade that could be made either green or red. She used the light as a taillight with the green showing, and from their position ahead of us the green light was all that could be seen. If ever that light went out, we were to stop. If ever it turned red, we were to turn around and head back from where we came.

I kept my eyes glued to that dancing light ahead, and peddled slowly beside Peter and Bish. Peter was whistling and I joined in with him, whistling, and trying to look Dutch whenever we passed anyone on the road. What a ride! One I'll certainly always remember. I held my breath when a glare of headlights pierced the darkness of the road and a German staff car sped by. Another.

Then a truck. Then we passed German soldiers walking along the road. Germans seemed to be all over, and I certainly wished I were already back in England

Quite abruptly, we came upon Mimi and her companion talking to a girl on a bicycle beside the road. We pulled up and Peter joined their conversation. Was this the girl we were to meet? Was everything all right? Peter turned and answered the question in our eyes with, "Let's go on. Everything is okay." Roelof's wife turned her bike and headed back the way we had come, waving good-bye over her shoulder. Again, Mimi, this time sitting behind the new girl, went ahead, and we followed behind as before until the arch that marked the start of the city loomed up in front.

The plan, evidently, was to rendezvous before entering the city and change our traveling arrangements. The girl with whom Mimi was riding surrendered her bicycle to Peter, and she walked off heading toward the arch. Peter and I followed. And Mimi walking alongside Bish, supporting him and pushing him as he tried to pedal with one foot, brought up the rear.

All the switching around happened fast, and neces-
sarily so, for all my dazed eyes could see were Germans,
here and everywhere. The city was lit up dimly with
truck headlights and cars, and looked to be teeming with
combat troops. I've since surmised that the troops were
probably massing in Meppel and in other locations
for the Battle of the Bulge, which was soon to come. I
followed Peter through the narrow streets. My heart was
pounding in my throat. Time and time again I had to
apply brakes to keep from running down Hitler's
supermen. I whistled softly as I went. Something very
tuneless, I thought, until it suddenly dawned on me that I
was whistling the popular U.S. song that went "Something, something (I can't remember the words) in Der
Fuhrer's face." I couldn't even think of anything else to
whistle except, for some reason, the "Lorelei." This was a
German song we had had on an old player piano roll
back home. I just stopped whistling and concentrated
on missing German soldiers.

Germans were everywhere. The streets were filled

with their cars and trucks. The sidewalks resounded to their stamping heels. I could have reached out and touched many as I was so close. I had one near miss. I "zigzagged" with a soldier, as sometimes happens with bicycles and pedestrians. The German soldier ended up straddling my front wheel. I couldn't say anything, but kept bobbing my head. He just laughed as I backed up and got around him. I had to smile to myself the way I was passing through their midst. The dumb jerks, if they noticed me at all, they just accepted me as another local Dutchman.

After several blocks we turned down a dark narrow side street. A motor convoy was parked along the curb, but with utter disregard, Peter shoved his bike between the trucks and through a gate, and I followed him along the side and around to the back of a brick house. We left our bikes, and entered through the back door into a darkened room. When the door was closed the overhead light was turned on. I blinked in its glare, and smiled at the middle-aged woman who greeted me and at another girl, who seemed to be in her early twenties. Almost immediately there was a tap on the door. The light was turned off, the door opened, and the girl who had met us on the road slipped in. I took a second look, for with the light, I saw a remarkably pretty girl in her teens with curly blond hair. Peter introduced us, and her name was Mientje. The other girl, also blond, but not nearly so attractive, Peter introduced as Jelly (pronounced Yelly) and the woman as Mevrouw, the Dutch word for Madam or Mrs.

We waited and waited, but still Mimi and Bish did not arrive. Peter began to look worried, and to glance impatiently from the window. What could have happened? It was easy to guess the worst, and all we could do was wait and pray and hope. Ah, there they were. I could hear Mimi speaking outside, and after the temporary dousing of the light the door opened and in they came. Bish hopping on one foot, his face pale with pain and excitement, and Mimi whistling in mock relief. It seems the strange arrangement of Bish riding and Mimi pushing had attracted some attention and they had gone far out of their way to escape anyone who may have followed them out of curiosity.

We had made it. All of us. The first step of our journey back. Could we make it all the way? I know now, but I didn't then. I could only hope.

CHAPTER 8

SURROUNDED

THE CITY OF MEPPEL, IN DECEMBER '44, WAS nothing more than a German garrison. A good third of the city was occupied by swarms of troopers. It seemed to me that in moving us to Meppel, a grave mistake had been made. I was further convinced that I was right, when I discovered our "safe" house was in the midst of the occupied section of town. Germans were everywhere. I could see them from every window. I knew that the houses nearby were all used to quarter my enemies. Behind our house, I was horrified to discover a German parade ground. It was separated from us by a low stone wall, and I watched as German soldiers in their baggy gray uniforms did close-order drill. Beyond the parade ground was the city's high school, now a barracks, and I certainly wished that the stone wall had been made considerably higher.

The house itself was great. It was fairly large, with several bedrooms, modern in Dutch style, and scrupulously clean. Mevrouw was a widow, and being left with two young children to support, she had been forced to turn her home into a boarding house. Whether all her boarders were Allied airmen, I do not know. But I do know how completely the woman hated the Germans.

She called them something that sounded like "Rot-muffs," rolling the "r" with a terrible vengeance. (I suspect that "Rottmuff" was a takeoff on Rottweiler, a German bred dog, similar to a German shepherd.) I never learned Mevrouw's story, but her hate for the Nazis was very apparent. The youngest of her children, a boy of four or five, stayed with friends away and apart from the possible disaster that clouded her home. The older, a girl of twelve, stayed with her mother and shared her danger. Jelly was a boarder who worked in the city, and she seemed to be the only person in the house not actively involved in the underground war against the Germans. But her very presence in the house and her association with the others gained her an equal share in the danger.

Mimi and Peter spoke fluent French and German. In addition, Peter spoke excellent English. They had been well educated in Rotterdam before the war. When Holland fell to the Germans, Peter, who had been in the Dutch army, had been taken prisoner. Due to his language skills he was not sent to a labor camp, but was given a job in the German controlled Dutch government. His job was to find and recruit Hollanders who had the needed skills to work in the occupying military government. He was assigned to the Meppel area, and like others working for the Germans he had special privileges and freedom to move about, even during curfew. Peter was also able to get Mimi a job as secretary to a high-ranking German officer in the local Labor Department.

What the Germans did not know was that they had hired two adamant Dutch patriots. They both were in position to obtain information useful to the Resistance groups and as Peter was highly placed in the area's Resistance organization, the information was put to good Dutch use. Peter, not the Peter known to the Germans, but the unknown man whose organization constantly caused disruption, was wanted badly, and a sentence of death was surely hanging over his head. But then execution, after merciless torture to extract information, was expected by all Hollanders caught in an act of sabotage or in aiding an enemy of the Germans.

Again, Bish and I shared a room, and gladly so, for it gave both of us a feeling of comfort knowing that we were not alone. The bathroom was on the first floor and we were surprised at Mimi's choice of words, when after showing us our room, she said, "If you have to shit or pee the head is downstairs." These words, although unladylike came out naturally. Obviously Mimi had learned them from prior escapees and had assumed they were proper American expressions.

In spite of my exciting and at times terrifying bike trip, I slept well that first night in Meppel. I'm afraid poor Bish, in contrast, spent another night racked with pain.

He barely closed his eyes the whole night. We rose together at a decent and civilized time, between 10:00 and 10:30, and went downstairs to see what our first day in town would bring. We had first washed using the pitcher of water and the washbowl in our room, and brushed our teeth with the wood handle toothbrushes we had been given. Boy, did that feel good! Even though we had to use regular soap for toothpaste.

Breakfast was waiting, and Mevrouw gave us some fresh coffee. Peter, as usual, was listening to his radio, which he had carried with him from Staphorst. He told us the BBC news and then settled back in his chair to give his undivided attention to the "B-bag," the GI swing program. When "B-bag" came on the air, Peter became completely absorbed. He was set adrift, floating by himself on a cloud of American jive. What a Dutchman! He was more American than I was.

That afternoon, a doctor arrived to look at Bish's foot. For just a sprain it was causing him an enormous amount of pain, and we were all afraid that he had broken a bone. Bish gritted his teeth as the doctor gave his foot a professional twist, and then broke into smiles when the verdict was pronounced. It was not broken, but just very badly sprained. A week or two would fix it up. A week or two! How long were we to remain in Mevrouw's house, surrounded as it was by Nazis? We had to be getting back. Getting back before we could be classified as "Missing in Action." Getting back before we would cause our folks more anxiety than they were already experiencing.

The doctor was a tall man with a fair complexion, and seemed awfully glad to see us. I guess we represented to him what he and every other Hollander wanted to be, an active soldier against the Third Reich. He could only fight in secret by using his skills to aid the Resistance. Never could he come out and face his enemy. But fight he would! Fight they all would till the day of their liberation.

The doctor thought he might have some good news for us, and through Peter, he told us that he had heard of another flyer somewhere in the vicinity who might be one of our crew. Boy, that was good news. But, eager as we were for more information, that was all he was able to tell us. However, he did promise that later that day he would attempt to find out where this other fellow was hiding and pay him a visit. Then he would bring us real first hand news. For my money, that guy was okay and soon perhaps we would know if another of our companions shared our good fortune.

The next morning, we were awakened early by Peter rapping on the bedroom door. He stood in the doorway, held a note up before our eyes, and said, "From Lieutenant Richard P. Fuller." Great guns! The other flyer in hiding was Dick! I had been praying that the doctor's unknown flyer would be one of our crew.

Peter tossed me the note, and I read aloud to Bish, what Dick saw fit to write. The tone of the note was just a little bit on the wary side, as if he didn't quite trust everybody. But, after I wrote him back, and we exchanged comments a few times, Dick and Bish and I were sure we were in the best of hands, and that everything was being done to speed our return.

The next few days in Meppel were busy ones. We were first measured for clothes by an elderly man who looked scared to death. Then after a bundle arrived the following day, we were "re-clothed" from head to foot in slightly used outer garments. We were fingerprinted. We were photographed. We were given new names, new occupations, new homes, ages and backgrounds. We were changed from American airmen to Dutch civilians in the course of those first few days. With my new identity I became a twenty-five-year-old medical intern, a graduate of Rotterdam University, working at present, under an old doctor in Staphorst. My new name was Peter Van Dussen, and I lived at some phony address in Staphorst and I was born in Utrecht. Loel Bishop had a similar identity change, and had some type of job associated with railroads. I wondered what I would do if I were ever asked some medical question. But then I wouldn't know it was a question unless it was asked in English, so why worry about an answer.

Day after day was spent studying Dutch words and pronunciation, and mastering phrases that might be necessary to pass through German roadblocks. Hopefully, as most German soldiers could not speak or understand Dutch, we might manage—unless unfortunately we met a

Dutch collaborator. Bish and I really tried hard to undergo our identity change, and the day finally came when Peter and Mimi became convinced we could get by. As graduation presents, Bish and I were presented with beautifully forged "German issued" Dutch passports, complete with our pictures and fingerprints, and were then officially Dutchmen.

During the days of our transformation, Mientje, the attractive blond courier for the Resistance, spent a good share of each day with us. She was as one of the household, and in spite of ourselves, both Bish and I formed more than a passing interest in her. We had many a good time trying to talk to her with the aid of an English-Dutch dictionary. She had an intriguing way of biting her lower lip when she showed surprise with our progress or when she was just happy.

Bish and I ate our evening meals with the Mrs. (we referred to her as Mrs. as we could not pronounce Mevrouw), her daughter, and Jelly, Mimi, and usually, Peter. Mimi lived in the house, like Jelly, as a boarder, but Peter would drop in often. Quite frequently he would

bring food. We ate well. The food was somehow expatri-
ated from German supplies and it was not the usual bread
and cheese eaten by German soldiers, but meat and potatoes, and once, even steak. Peter would laugh and say,
"The Rottmuffs will never miss it." The Mrs. was a good
cook, and I was surprised to see that her boarders put
some of everything on their plates and then mixed all
together before eating. Bish and I still ate this and then
that, savoring the flavors, and didn't follow the apparent
Dutch style of mixing it all together.

Day after day slipped by, and despite the combined
efforts of Peter and the girls, Bish and I grew more and
more anxious to start moving toward freedom.
December was fast running out of days, and so were our
hopes of spending Christmas back in England. Peter was
doing his best with daily meetings and communications,
trying to hurry preparations for our escape. Bish and I
tried to keep calm and patient, but in spite of the books,
the radio, and the little pump organ, each of us was constantly on edge. Looking back now, I can see how foolish
we were not to enjoy those days to the fullest. They were

rather nice and seemingly carefree. I can remember the night I tried to teach the girls and Peter to jitterbug (the dance craze in America). They were interested pupils, but clumsy and, boy, how ungraceful. Solid Dutchmen is a good description.

Then there was the day Bish, Peter, and I attempted to chop down a dead tree in the backyard. I say attempted, for neither Peter nor I had ever really used an axe and our efforts were pretty useless. Old "Tex" Bishop, a real honest to God ranch-hand, had felled many a tree in his eighteen years, and with little effort added this one to his score. Yes, those days were happy ones, if not carefree, but every night as we lay in bed, we would speculate on our chances of getting back. The iron heels of our German neighbors ringing up from the street below our window, only served to heighten our concern.

Perhaps in this house, in the midst of a German garrison, we were perfectly safe. Personally, I felt no such assurance. Our visit to the backyard to cut down a dead tree was, I thought, ridiculous to say the least, even dressed as we were in Dutch clothing. Disaster was impending. I could feel it coming. Too many people were involved in our welfare. Every day it seemed we were in contact with new faces, and new tongues that might slip. Peter would only laugh when I told him how I felt. He would say, "It's a big club. These people are okay." What could I do but accept his answer. The show was in his hands.

I did keep reminding Peter that something should be done about the emergency hiding place. I knew it was no good. Bish knew it was no good. But day after day everyone else went blissfully on assuming it would provide adequate protection if and when needed. Why? Because it had never been used—never been given the "acid" test—and so never proved worthless.

What a hiding place! As usual, just a trap door to a space beneath the floor. The most common of all places to hide, but far worse than its being common, was that the trap door was beneath the carpet just a few feet from the front door. Somehow, I couldn't see Bish and myself leaping from bed, rushing silently down the stairs, slipping under the floor, closing the trap door, having someone replace the carpet, all while Storm Troopers were pounding on the front door with their pistols. It wasn't practical, and finally, we made the rest see our point of view. Peter promised to bring some tools the next day, and we could begin work on something better. At last, we had roused him from that false feeling of security he seemed to have. For anyone risking his life as he was, indifference could be deadly.

It was noon the next day before we began work on our new hiding place. The morning had been spent in collecting tools and planning our work. We had selected a really perfect place to hide, and even better, one with a more convenient entrance. We discovered that directly below the floor of our upstairs wardrobe was a downstairs room partition. The partition was thicker than usual and it already contained between its sides a motorbike and other valuables. These were plastered in before the fall of Holland and the German occupation. We planned to make the floor of the wardrobe removable, and to use it as an entrance to the same space. It would be a tight squeeze, but perfect for our use.

That afternoon, we removed the floor molding in the closet and started to saw the thick floorboards. We worked steadily and carefully, trying to do a job that could not be detected. The hours wore on, and darkness fell before we had quite finished our work. It was too difficult to see, so we left our tools and the "almost finished" job for the light of the following day. If we had known what was to come, we would have labored on in the dark, for it was nothing compared to the night of "blackness" that would soon fall upon us. But how were we to know what was to come? For twelve days, we had successfully evaded capture. Why was one more night so important? How were we to know?

While Bish and I were working on the new hiding place, the Mrs. decided it was time to wash our "long-johns" and socks. Evidently, our constant wear, day and night, had resulted in a bit of an odor that we had grown accustomed to and did not notice. The Mrs., smiling and holding her nose, took our underclothes and socks to her laundry, leaving each of us with only a cotton shirt and the baggy Dutch style pants and a belt. We still had our ordinary looking escape shoes, but without any socks to fill them out.

Peter arrived that evening, as usual, with a bottle of Genever, ready to party. Genever frequently brightened up our evenings. It's a clear, potent Dutch gin. Pretty raw to drink straight, like good Dutchmen were supposed to do. The girls, Mimi, Jelly and the Mrs. would add a little sugar. I am not sure what the occasion was, but Peter was in exceptionally good spirits. Probably, he had outwitted the Germans again and he insisted we finish the bottle. He was also staying later, it was approaching ten o'clock, but then again the curfew never seemed to bother him as he pretty well came and went as he pleased. I imagine his government job provided him with a special German endorsed pass.

CHAPTER 9

CAPTURED

IT WAS A LITTLE AFTER 10:00 WHEN OUR gathering was interrupted by a tremendous pounding on the front door. German style pounding. Not a simple knock. We looked at each other. The Mrs. looked terrified. Peter signaled Bish and me to go upstairs. There wasn't time to get under the floor by the front door as the pounding was shaking the door and locks. We dashed upstairs and Peter who was following us dove under our bed. Bish and I crammed into the wardrobe we had been working on, and tried to hide behind the clothes. Our carpenter tools were still on the floor.

We heard the Mrs. opening the door, and then the

guttural shouting of Germans. There were sounds of heavy boots tramping all over the first floor, of doors being opened and slammed shut, of furniture being knocked over, and dishes and glasses crashing on the floor. We heard Mimi and the Mrs. trying to speak, and the sounds of vicious slaps and hysterical crying.

Soldiers pounded up the stairs, and burst into our room. We heard the bed flipped up and the scraping sound of Peter being dragged out. There were muffled blows, lots of shouting and Peter's gasps. The closet door was pulled open, and Bish was seen immediately and yanked out. I stayed in the back behind the clothes, with my heart pounding, but hoping against hope that they would be satisfied with finding just one. It was so obvious that we would be in the closet, but when we dashed upstairs it was any port in a storm, and it was really a terrifying storm.

There was continuous shouting, the noise numbing my mind, and then a shot was fired in the floor by my feet. There was a sudden silence and someone started counting, "ein, zwei." It was in German, but I knew that much German and "three" was coming next. I pushed through the hanging clothes and out of the closet with my hands in the air.

There were several German soldiers in the room, and Peter and Bish were on the floor, face down with their hands behind their heads. The soldiers had skull and crossbones on their hats—the symbol of the dreaded SS, Hitler's elite troops—the tough guys, who did the dirty work for the Gestapo. Next to the soldier with his Luger pointing at me was an ugly looking trooper with several stripes on his tunic. He pushed me back against the door-jamb, and swung a fist at my face. Instinctively, I pulled my head to the side, and his fist smashed hard into the wood. I thought then and there I would be killed, but just then a pasty-faced civilian in a double-breasted gray suit stepped into the room shouting something. The guy with the gun pointed to the insignia on his hat and shouted, "SS, SS," as if it were to put additional terror in my heart. The soldier, shaking the obvious pain out of his hand, shouted and pointed to the floor and I quickly joined Peter and Bish in their prone positions.

The civilian started back down the stairs. More shouting below and then steady machine gun fire. With trembling hands, we had to take the laces out of our shoes and they were used to tie our hands behind our backs. We were taken downstairs where Mimi was huddled in a corner, and the Mrs. was lying in a pool of blood. The poor, brave woman . . . dead because she tried to help us. The walls of the living room had been shot full of holes, and we also would have been full of holes if we had been in our new hiding place.

There was what appeared to me total confusion, but I did not see Jelly or the Mrs.' daughter. I hoped they had slipped out the back door and away in the darkness before the Germans pounded into the house.

The three of us, Peter, Bish, and I were taken out of the house and marched down the street. We were surrounded by five or six SS guards, and when I tried to tell Bish we would be okay, "Sprechen Nicht. Sprechen Verboten," was shouted at me by one of the guards. Obviously I wasn't to talk. The street was dark except for the guards' flashlights, and walking, or rather shuffling, with untied shoes over the cobblestones was difficult. Also, it was cold. The December night breeze whipped right through our shirts, but I knew that my shivering was not only from the cold but also from the fear of what was to come.

We eventually arrived at a two-story brick building and were escorted by our guards into the lobby. Bish and I were taken to a large room at the end of the hall. Peter was shoved into the adjacent room. Looking around our room, which was lighted but had shuttered windows, we saw several disheveled men sitting or laying on the floor. There were SS guards sitting at a desk in the corner by the door. A radio was playing in the next room, and I remember hearing Bing Crosby singing "White Christmas." An elderly man, small, with white hair stained with blood, was standing facing the wall. He looked familiar, and I recognized him as the postman whom I had seen delivering mail to the Mrs.' house. He had been severely beaten, and the inside of his left ear was protruding fully an inch from his head. It looked like bloody pulp. He was moaning and leaning his head against the wall.

The guards produced two straight-backed chairs for Bish and me, and we were told by gesture to sit down. They asked, "Americans?" And we nodded in agreement. They untied our hands and gave us back our shoelaces, but shouted "Sprechen nicht" when we tried to talk.

The music from the radio was a mixture of Christmas music and German marches, periodically blotted out by the shouts and laughter of the Germans in the adjacent room. We could only guess what was happening in that room. We could hear muffled sounds and then feel the wall shake as without doubt Peter was thrown against it. The muffled sounds of steady beating, with Christmas carols for background was an unimaginable combination. Christmas was the time for good will to man, but the beating continued. I could only pray that Peter would survive the rest of the night.

The door to our room was thrown open, and Mimi and Mientje were brought in. Mimi could barely walk and her face was red and puffy. Mientje looked terrified, and I wondered how they got hold of her, as she was not with us when we were captured. Bish and I got up to give them our chairs, but Mimi just put her finger to her lips and shook her head. I had to assume that we were not to speak to them or indicate that we were acquainted. Mimi and Mientje sat on the floor in the corner next to our chairs. Mimi clasped her knees to her chin and rested her head and moaned softly as the wall trembled—and Peter's beating continued.

Morning finally came. The beating had stopped. The old man was still on his feet, as every time he slid to the floor, the guards shouted him up. Soon, two SS men came for Bishop and me. Our turn? How would I hold up under torture? Name, rank and serial number was all I could give. There was nothing else I knew. We had been evading capture for twelve days and any military information I might have had was certainly out of date. Peter and Mimi had been very careful to tell us nothing specific about where we had been staying or the last names of any of the people who had been helping us. I felt a little comfort in knowing that there was nothing of importance that could be beaten out of us.

As we were taken down the hall, the pasty-faced

civilian in the gray suit came out of the room where Peter had been taken. I gathered he was either a Gestapo agent or a Dutch collaborator. I can shut my eyes now and visualize his face. A face I will probably never forget.

Bish and I were taken up a flight of stairs to a room on the second floor. There we were greeted by a couple of SS troopers in a rather friendly way. They kept saying, "Americans, essen" and gave each of us a sandwich of black bread and bacon—"raw" bacon. Trichinosis or not we gobbled them down, although initially my stomach churned at the raw, uncooked taste. They even gave us a cup of coffee.

After we finished eating, they accompanied us to the bathroom and then took us back downstairs. As we turned the landing to the lower flight, we saw Mientje. She was on her hands and knees, scrubbing the stairs. Tears were running down her face—a scared little girl. She didn't look at us and we never saw her again. I hope God took care of her and that she survived.

We did not go back to the room where we had spent the sleepless night. We were taken outside. Snow had fallen and we were marched through the slushy streets to a small one-story brick building sandwiched between other similar buildings. The building we were herded into had a "Polizei" sign over the door. It looked to me like the Meppel city jail, and that's what it was. Inside was a receiving counter and a long corridor lined with cells for prisoners. The cells were small, and in each cell door there was a little rectangular opening at eye level. Bish and I were taken down the corridor by our guards to the last cell in the row. It was already filled with civilian prisoners. They were sitting or lying on the floor and there was really no room for the two of us.

The guards said something about Americans and shoved us inside. The other men, who were Dutch, and in jail for whatever reasons, stared at us and started talking, "Americans? American pilots?" And then they made space for us to sit down on the floor. They treated us as if we were great heroes. One, who could speak a bit of English, said, "You help our country. Thank you. Thank you. Thank you," or words to that effect. It was embarrassing as by now we were convinced that the Dutch, not us, were the real heroes in this our unplanned, unfortunate visit to their country.

We spent four or five days in that cell. The civilian prisoners were regularly taken out and replaced by others. I assumed the cell was a "holding tank" for prisoners being held temporarily for minor civilian type offenses. Bish and I were wary of the new additions who might possibly be German collaborators, and we were careful in our talk to each other.

Once a day, in the evening, we were given a meager ration of bread and soup and then taken to the latrine. The jail was run by the Dutch who were obviously sympathetic to our situation, but there were always German soldiers hanging around to keep everyone in line.

It was probably mid-afternoon when Bish and I were taken out of the cell for our next move. Through the front window of the building I could see that it was still daylight. We had had nothing to eat or drink since the previous evening so the quick stop we made at the latrine was not all that necessary. We were then led along the hall and I saw Mimi sitting by the receiving counter. It looked liked she was tied to her chair, as her arms were stretched behind the chair in an awkward position. The last cell door, the one nearest to the counter, was open. I looked inside as we passed and I saw what I believed was Peter. The man I saw wore only pants and his body was dark purple from the waist up. His feet were bloody, and his face was beaten beyond recognition. Only his blond hair and general build let me identify him as the happy-go-lucky Peter of a few days ago. "God, take care of him," I whispered. I was certain that like the Mrs., he and Mimi would soon be executed. I was also certain that the Nazis had learned nothing from Peter, or Mimi. They were great people. I was so fortunate to have known them.

CHAPTER 10

CHRISTMAS IN JAIL

A DUTCH POLICEMAN HAD TAKEN US FROM our crowded cell, first to the latrine and then down the hall to the front door by the receiving counter. Waiting at the front door were two SS troopers. They tied our hands behind our backs, and pushed us, not too gently, into the back seat of a German army four-door sedan. The two troopers got into the front and we drove off. I guess we were heading north, but I'm not sure. We did drive for quite some time, and it became almost too dark to see. We were thirsty, hungry, and worried. Every attempt we made to talk to each other was shouted down. We had no idea of what to expect next—especially since we were yet to be interrogated.

Later in the evening, we arrived at some kind of military installation. Barrack type buildings could be seen in the subdued headlights of the car, and people were milling around. We were taken inside a building for a few minutes, while the SS guards talked to a German officer. The officer called other soldiers who then took us outside, and walked us a short distance through freshly fallen snow and slush. We headed toward what appeared to be a long bunker built half in and half out of the ground. We were taken down a few steps to an entrance that was below ground level. Inside was a long dark corridor lit only by the soldiers' flashlights. There were heavy wooden doors along one side. About the third or fourth door down the corridor, the soldiers opened the door, untied my hands and shoved me inside. Before the door was closed cutting off light from the flashlights, I saw I was in a small room with a wooden platform on one side. The room had a dirt floor, a small barred window high in the opposite wall, and when the door closed behind me, I could see light from the flashlights through a small louver in the door. Bish, obviously, was taken to a similar room. I heard his door slammed and locked, and the soldiers walking back down the hall.

The room, or rather my cell, had no light. The little window looked out on a pitch-black night, and there was no glass to keep out the cold air. I stood with my back flattened against the door. I could faintly hear a radio playing the hymn "Silent Night, Holy Night." "My God," I thought, "this is Christmas Eve." Shivers of cold spread through me, and my body shook in uncontrollable spasms, a feeling I could hardly believe. "Round yon Virgin, Mother and Child." The coarse voices of my guards could be heard as they sang along with the music from the radio.

I stared into the darkness of my cell. My eyes ached from trying to see. I felt my way along the walls until I came in contact with the wooden platform. It was the only place I found on which I could sit or lay down. I lay down on the wood and pulled my knees up under my chin. My hands were freezing and I squeezed them tight between my thighs. There was no blanket, no warmth.

I had received food (I guess you could call it food) from my keepers when they first shoved me into that dark hole, which I unfortunately soon had to foul with my own mess. They had thrown a heel of stale bread in after me before slamming shut the door. Groping around the floor, I had found it. I wiped it off on my shirt, and had to spit on it to soften it to eat—my Christmas Eve dinner. I almost had to laugh as I bit into its moldy hardness. I should have cried. It was funny, but I could not laugh either. I just lay on the shelf. My hip started to ache from the hard wood. I turned over. The shelf lurched when I moved, and something scuttled from underneath. I couldn't see it; I couldn't see anything. Probably a German rat. "Sleep in heavenly peace." Christmas. Hell.

I wondered what my folks were doing as I lay on my bed hugging myself for warmth. It was Christmas Eve. It had to be. I'd arrived in the evening, but it was so dark it may have been after midnight and already Christmas. I may have slept. I don't think so. I was probably there only a few hours, but it seemed like an eternity. "The night before Christmas, all through the house" kept running through my frostbitten brain. At home the Christmas tree would have been standing in the living room looking pretty and kind of warm. I thought I would just pretend, just a little, that I was home. Just like a little kid, I would pretend. Nobody would know; I was all alone.

Then by gosh, my body shook with a real sob. I knew I would have to control my emotions. There was no point in feeling sorry for myself. Thinking of Christmas and home was dangerous, but I couldn't help myself.

When dinner was over and it was dark outside, I would, as a little kid, crawl behind the Christmas tree and plug in the cord to turn on the colored lights. When Mom and Sis were through with the dishes it was time to open presents. I wondered if the gifts I sent home from England were there. I sent them early, but with a war going on who knows how long it may have taken for them to arrive.

The guards' radio was turned up louder as German marches were being played. Dishes were rattling as the guards sang and pounded the table to the beat. I remember shouting, "Shut up, you sons-of-bitches, you bastards. Let me out of here." My voice echoed in my cell, to my ears only. Gee I was cold.

I was so cold. What should I do? What would happen to me? There were rats all around. I kept my feet up on the wooden bed. I wondered if my hand would freeze if I used it as a pillow for my head. My ears were throbbing, probably frostbitten. I wondered if I would ever see daylight again, or would I just freeze to death in my sleep. I prayed for help and for my folks. I kept visualizing the Christmas tree. My brain must have been getting numb. The guards switched from banging their tin cups in time to the marches and began to sing Christmas carols. Eventually I slept. It was daylight when I awoke. Light was coming in through the little window in the cell, and I quickly snapped back to reality. I was stiff, freezing cold, and starving. I walked back and forth in my prison, trying to get feeling back into my legs and feet. I was sure my toes were frostbitten. The shoes without socks provided no warmth, nor did my cotton shirt and baggy pants.

The day wore on, and I heard my guards coming down the hall. They stopped at my door and shoved a tray with food through the small louver! My Christmas dinner—cold Brussels sprouts, a slice of bread, and a cup of horrible tasting coffee. I gulped it all down even though I was pretty sure the Brussels sprouts were at the turning point of being spoiled.

My solitary confinement continued day after day after day. A week went by, maybe more. A week of shivering, starving, and talking to myself. Once I heard the drone of high flying aircraft, and looking out at the sky through my little window, I saw the contrails of a B-17 formation high over head. Was it my group? How I wished I was up there, with my crew, flying with them.

Once a day, the guards would take me to a latrine inside the bunker. I could speak to the guards, but received no replies to my questions. I could find out nothing about Bish, but I had heard him in the hall on his "once a day" latrine trip. The unresponsive guards provided my only human contact, and I was going slowly batty, just sitting, mostly in the dark, all alone with only my thoughts.

CHAPTER 11

THE INTERROGATION

EVENTUALLY, AFTER MANY DAYS—I'M NOT sure how many—I was taken out of the cell and to the outside. Bish joined me and together we were marched on our wobbly legs towards the open front gate of the compound. Two guards with light machine guns and two others in heavy coats prodded us forward. Bish looked horrible. Pale, dirty, unshaven, with tangled hair. I'm sure that I looked just as bad to him. At least we were able to say a few words to each other before the usual, "Sprechen Nicht."

Beyond the open gate a car was waiting to take us on

our next trip to God knows where. As we headed towards the car the guards lagged behind. Bish whispered to me, "This is it Skipper, I can feel it." I had similar thoughts. It seemed we were being set up to be gunned down, and it would look like we were trying to escape. That was foolish as we were both so weak and cold that we could hardly shuffle along, but the fear was there and we both expected the end with every step. Then with relief we realized it was not as we feared, the guards had just slowed down to light cigarettes and to talk. We reached the car and the guards with the guns opened the back door and shoved us in.

The car was a sedan equipped with a charcoal burner built into the trunk. The methane gas from the burning charcoal, stored in what looked like a hot water tank, provided the fuel to the engine. The two soldiers in the heavy coats sat in the front, and we started on our way. They were not SS, and were probably regular army types. They didn't bother to tie our hands as before. Probably we looked too weak and pitiful to cause them any concern. I know we envied their heavy wool coats, as Bish and I were still shivering, although we were getting used to being half, or all frozen.

I believe we were moving toward the German border. It was morning, and we seemed to be heading east. The car ran fairly well on the charcoal gas, but not too fast. Every once in a while, we stopped, and one of the soldiers would stoke up the charcoal fire for more fuel for the engine.

Around noon, we stopped at a house in a small town—a German town. Unbelievably, we were fed. The lady of the house and her husband gave each of us a bowl containing a jelly-like stew. It was warm and oh so good, after days of practically nothing but black bread and watery soup. Our guards had the same fare, and they laughed and talked to the lady and the man as they ate. They were certainly different from Hitler's arrogant SS troopers. Bish and I were also able to talk a bit to each other, and compare notes on our last ordeal. Our treatment had been pretty much the same. Bish's ankle was considerably better, and he could walk with less of a limp.

Late in the afternoon, we arrived at what appeared to be an old warehouse in a small city. We were taken up a wooden flight of stairs to a large loft. Several other prisoners were there—a Norwegian, with wings on his tunic, an Australian, and a few English soldiers. No Americans. Along one wall there were a number of straw-filled mattresses. The other prisoners were sitting or lying on the mattresses watching us, but not speaking until our guards left and went back down the stairs. We joined the group, and for the first time since our capture, we could talk openly. The others all had tales of hardship at the hands of the Germans, and all had been in the loft for several days.

The Norwegian could not speak English, but when he determined, in spite of our lack of uniforms and "raunchy" appearance, that we were American Airmen, he smiled and gave us a thumbs-up sign. The Australian was a glider pilot. His tow plane had been shot down and he had no choice but to glide his ship, filled with supplies, to the ground and the waiting Germans.

The one disturbing sight that constantly attracted our

eyes were two six-foot-high posts at the head of the stairs. The posts were splintered, chunks of wood were missing, and they were splattered with what appeared to be dried blood. In front of the posts were two machine gun tripods, but no guns. The purpose was all too clear, but the other prisoners had no first hand knowledge of their use.

We still had no blankets or warm clothing, but Bish and I lay down on our straw mattresses with great relief. The straw was a tremendous improvement over the bare wooden planks of our previous jail. I could feel sore spots all over my body from the days and days of lying on that unforgiving, rigid board surface. The only drawback to my mattress was feeling little bodies moving around under the ticking and in the straw. Just friendly little mice trying to stay warm. On the opposite wall, however, rats—German rats—could be seen moving unconcernedly along the ledge below the roofline. It wasn't a great place to stay, and for how long, I had no clue. I was still freezing from the incessant cold.

Finally, I was interrogated. No one had asked me a

thing since the first day of our capture. Now it seemed to be my turn. I was taken downstairs to a room where a German officer sat behind a desk. Other soldiers were standing by. I remember the officer's rimless glasses as he stared at me in an unfriendly way. He motioned for me to sit down on a chair facing his desk, just like the war movies I had seen. But this was no movie. Here I was in civilian clothes, carrying false Dutch papers, and with a false name. I was a prime candidate for treatment as a spy. I could feel beads of sweat on my forehead as I looked into those unfriendly eyes.

His questions were initially straightforward, like "Just who are you?" He was looking at my Dutch identification card, and at my U.S. Army card, both of which had evidently arrived with me. My answer was simple—name, rank and serial number. He laughed and told me exactly who I was. He also knew my aircraft and where and when I was shot down. Obviously, all this was known from where I was taken prisoner and from the vicinity where most of my crew had been captured. Then he shouted questions at me about where had I been for the past weeks? And whom I was with. Thank God that I really did not know. Except for the city of Meppel where I was captured, I had no specific knowledge of where I had been. And as no one had ever told me anyone's full name, I really did not know the people who had helped me along the way. I felt confident that name, rank and serial number would get me by unless my lack of uniform would be my undoing.

The officer shouted at me in German and in French and then in perfect English. He wanted more, but I had nothing to tell. He didn't ask anything relating to the mission I was flying or what I might know about my group, and that sort of thing. His questions actually told me things that up to then I did not know. I gathered he was trying to find out if I had some other reasons for being in Holland. Again, my attire and fake ID were my stumbling blocks. The shouting in German and one hard whack on the side of my head, by the guard behind me, was pretty well the extent of the so-called interrogation.

The officer and guards kept talking together and kept watching me. Then I was pulled from my chair and taken back up the stairs. At the top of the stairs the guards pushed me against one of the bloody posts and tied my arms behind it. I was sure this was it for me. All that was needed was to mount a gun on the tripod. I could see Bish watching in utter horror from his mattress, and I could feel my legs trembling. More shouting in German, and then the officer who had followed us up the stairs started to laugh. "You are too stupid to be a spy," he said. "You don't understand German. You don't understand Dutch or French. You haven't understood a word of what we have been saying." The guards untied me then, and gave me a push toward the back of the loft. And, on legs almost too limp to carry my weight, I walked back to my mattress, and I dropped to my knees, and then onto my back, saying in my heart, "Thank you, Lord Jesus. Thank you. Thank you."

CHAPTER 12

ESCAPE ATTEMPT

WE LEARNED FROM OUR NEW COMPANIONS IN the warehouse that the German Army had initiated a major offensive directed at Belgium. I know now that this was the "Battle of the Bulge", and the build-up for the offensive was probably why there were so many German troops in and around Meppel. It was those troops that delayed and prevented our escape towards Allied lines and back to England. I hoped that this was a last ditch effort by the Nazis, and that our guys would quickly roll the Wehrmacht (the German regular 'GI' army) back into Germany. News of the offensive was obviously not the kind of news Bish and I wanted to hear,

but the Australian glider pilot told us he had been fer-
rying supplies to paratroopers that were part of an Allied
counteroffensive that was apparently gathering steam.

The strategic thinking of a twenty-two-year-old Lieutenant, whose only military training was in flying heavy
bombers, is not too great; and so I started to think
seriously of what Peter had told me might be a possible
option for our return to Allied control. That option, a last
ditch option, was for Bish and me to hide in some safe
place near the front lines where we could stay and wait
for the Allies to over-run our position. I knew that with
the slow speed of our last trip, in the car that ran on
charcoal, we could not be very far inside Germany. I also
knew that we had been traveling south and so could be
fairly close to where this new action was taking place. I
had a wild idea that if we could get out of this warehouse
we could execute that last ditch option by hiding on some
farm, or someplace, and just wait a few days for rescue by
our forces. I also had been feeling awfully guilty that I
was doing nothing to escape and was letting my country
down. Reason told me that was not the case, as since my

capture I had absolutely no opportunity to take any action. I was still shivering incessantly from the cold and felt as weak as a kitten. Days of hiding somewhere, without food or water was not going to help my condition one little bit. Regardless, I felt I had to try, and to do so before the Germans changed their minds and completed what they started to do when they tied me to that post.

For starters I would investigate how well the place was guarded. There were no soldiers watching us in the loft, and outside of our visit to the latrine and my stint in the downstairs interrogation room, I had no idea what was on the floor below. I would do a little scouting after dark. I would reconnoiter alone and not drag Bish into anything that I might regret.

I was curled up in my usual position, trying to keep warm, while I waited for the others to fall asleep. The loft was dimly lit by a couple of low-wattage bulbs hanging from the ceiling and I had no way of telling time as my watch had long since been taken from me. I suspected that it was close to midnight as only blackness could be seen through the cracks in the wooden walls. I waited and waited until all was quiet and I sensed no activity from the floor below. I slipped off my shoes and crept silently towards the stairs, as I didn't want any of my comrades calling out to see what was going on. I reached the stairs and started down.

The warehouse had high ceilings and the stairs had a mid-point landing and a right angle turn to the lower floor. I waited on the landing for some time looking for any guards. The lower floor was well lit in comparison to the loft and I had a partial view of the lower hall. There was movement and I saw a guard. He was standing just inside the doorway of an open room. The doorway was parallel to the stairs and about ten feet away. The guard had his back to me and was watching whatever was going on in the room. It probably was a card game as there was occasional conversation, the rustle of cards and now and then a chuckle. I saw no other guards. I should have quit right then and there and gone back upstairs, but with my heart pounding I descended the steps and slipped off to the left and away from the guard and the open door.

The hall was lighted and I stayed in the shadow of the

stairs. I headed towards the front and to the only door I could see to the outside. It was a large warehouse door and appeared to be well secured with a huge old-fashioned key lock. There was no possible way out through that door, and so I started creeping along the hall still keeping in the shadow of the stairs. There were several rooms all with their doors shut and locked. I tested each in turn by turning the knobs to see if they would open. There was one darkened room with the door open. It was the lavatory. I could see a lighter spot from its only window high up on the far wall. It was small but maybe that window was a way out.

I never got a chance to check it further, for just then the bell that was hanging over the front door started to clang. Cripes, someone wanted in! I had only seconds before the guard would come into the hall, and looking wildly around I ducked into the lavatory and into the nearest officers' toilet stall with its privacy door. I heard the guard open the front door and the boisterous voices of several soldiers as they came in. Then my heart almost stopped beating as they came into the lavatory and switched on the overhead lights. With my mind racing like mad, I pulled down my pants and sat on the toilet. Perhaps I could use the need to go as an excuse for being downstairs. With perspiration running off my forehead and my nose, I waited for the inevitable.

It didn't happen. The soldiers evidently relieved themselves and left, flipping off the lights. I waited until I could breathe more or less normally, and slipped out of the room. I had done a foolish thing, but at least I knew that there was no easy way out, even considering the little window that was too high up in the lavatory wall for us to reach. Now all I had to do was to get back upstairs.

Again luck was with me, for the soldiers who had just returned obviously had stories to tell to their comrades. The stair guard was well inside the room at the foot of the stairs, enjoying the conversation. I got up to the landing undetected. I then crept up the second flight to the loft and found all my fellow prisoners sitting up watching me arrive. So much for stealth! We didn't dare speak, but I brought them up to date in the morning. I didn't get to sleep for hours. I guess I probably was too excited.

CHAPTER 13

THE AIR RAID

SEVERAL DAYS PASSED BY, AND MORE CAP-
tives were brought into the loft. They were British and
Canadian soldiers. All were in uniform. Bish and I, again
because of our civilian clothes, received questioning
stares from the new arrivals until they were told that
we were American flyers captured while trying to get
back to Allied territory. The new arrivals were all taken
prisoner in the Battle of the Bulge, but they had little
information on how things were going. In retrospect,
Bish and I could also blame our capture on that offensive,
even though it didn't start until some time after we had
dropped into Holland. The German troops were there in

138

and around our escape route, and the massing of troops was probably the reason Peter was not optimistic about our quick return to England.

A day or two after the British and Canadians joined us we were all herded out of the building. It was early morning, and two army trucks were waiting at the front door. We tried to ask where we were going, and as usual, no one answered our questions. When we were out of the city, the trucks separated, and our truck, with just the "airmen types," continued in an easterly direction.

After several hours of bumping around on the floor of the truck we arrived at our destination and were unloaded in a railroad marshaling yard on the edge of what looked like a fairly good size city. It was about mid-afternoon, and there were civilian workers and travelers milling around.

Suddenly, the air was shattered with a loud wailing. An air raid siren. It went on and on, and people began to run toward a brick building further down the tracks. It was the Frankfurt railroad station, I later found out, and our guards rushed us, as a group, toward the building. I could hear the low drone of high-flying bombers, and way up I could see the contrails of the formation. When we reached the building, we were rushed down a couple flights of stairs to a lower level. People were gathering, and were obviously very frightened. They kept staring at us, and muttering. It was scary as obviously there was no love for us at that time.

Soon I heard the rattle of bomb fins, and then explosion after explosion. It was frightening. Being in a bomb raid looking "up" rather than "down" was an experience I'd rather not repeat. The people were terrified as the explosions continued, and the looks they gave us were getting more and more menacing.

After a seemingly endless time the explosions stopped and the sirens sounded the "all clear." There was smoke and fire all around, but the damage seemed to be concentrated mainly in the marshaling area and the railroad car repair and storage sheds.

In spite of the confusion, we were loaded and locked in a boxcar. We sat there for what seemed an endless amount of time, and then the door was opened and freshly downed airmen—American Airmen—were shoved in. Some were limping and were being helped by others, and there were some with fresh bloody bandages. After an hour or so, the car finally was hooked up to an engine and we were again on our way. Wherever "our way" was.

The next day we reached our destination. It was not far away from the bombed railroad station, and when I saw that our new guards were wearing Luftwaffe insignia, I realized that Bish and I had finally been transferred from the SS, via the German army, to the German air force, the Luftwaffe.

We were marched along the tracks to a big camp with a number of brick buildings inside a wire-enclosed area. We were herded into one of the buildings, which seemed to contain nothing but steel doors leading to small cells. There was no room sharing, and when the door to my cell was slammed behind me, I realized I was alone again.

There was no window to the outside, but there was a small window-like opening in the door. The room was lit by a light bulb in the ceiling that never was turned off, and equipped with the usual wooden shelf for a bed. But oh, great joy, on the bed was a pad and a blanket. With still only a cotton shirt and baggy pants in the middle of January, that blanket was a true "Godsend." I got all wrapped up in the blanket, and lay down on my wooden bed. I was almost warm except for the chill I felt being all alone. More solitary? I didn't know. If I was in for another siege of the emptiness that was solitary confinement, I might just go around the bend. But it couldn't be worse than that underground cell. Here, at least, there was light, and a blanket.

The tapping started. Tap. Tap, tap, tap, tap. Tap, tap to the rhythm of that childish jingle—"Shave and a hair cut, two bits." It was coming through the wall. I tapped back, and then a faint voice asked, "Who are you?" To answer, I was not sure whether to shout or to whisper. I tried whispering first, and then louder until the voice answered back. My answer was, "I'm an American flyer." A kind of a generic type response to someone I didn't know. And then I asked, "Where am I?" The answer, "Dulag Luft"— the infamous Dulag Luft. It was well known to all of us as the Luftwaffe's Central Interrogation Center and it was located in Oberursel, near Frankfurt. We had all been briefed on Dulag Luft and knew what to expect. The Luftwaffe was reasonably civilized, and probably there would be no beatings. The voice through the wall said he too was an American flyer, and based on his experience, I could count on staying where I was for a while. I knew from the briefing that I would eventually be sent to a prisoner of war camp.

Food was delivered once a day and was scarcely worth eating. But, as I was steadily being starved to death, or so it seemed to me, I looked forward to the daily serving of bread and broth. The days wore on, one after another. Days of solitaire and loneliness. Never was asked a question. Never saw another person outside of the guard. My neighbor, who had tapped on the wall, was evidently gone, and again I lost track of time and my thoughts were only of the past.

I was so concerned about my Mom and Dad. They had lost my brother to diphtheria before I was born and they never seemed to get over their grief. Now I was adding to it. My concern, my guilt for being where I was, my every thought, made me feel more and more like I was losing my mind.

The day finally came when I was taken from my cell, and out of the building. I expected it was finally interrogation time for me. Instead, several of us were loaded into a truck and driven to another nearby compound. The compound had a number of barrack type wooden buildings and several separately fenced-in areas. The whole compound was surrounded by barbed wire fencing with guard towers and searchlights. It was still part of Dulag Luft and I learned a bit later that it was the gathering place for prisoners in transit to permanent POW camps.

I was taken to one of the buildings where a civilian with a Red Cross armband told me in English that I was to take a shower and then I would get some warmer clothes. Wow! What a relief. Relief for not having to face a Dulag Luft interrogation and relief at the prospect of truly getting clean. I showered, but with only a minute or two of hot water, it was the fastest shower I had ever taken. But I was clean again. The Red Cross representative then gave me new long underwear—tops and bottoms, and a pair of wool socks. The underwear was through the courtesy of the International Red Cross. Then he showed me a pile of used clothes. I picked out a pair of British wool army pants, a GI shirt, and a British wool uniform jacket. I wondered about the fate of the poor soldiers who had contributed to that pile of clothes.

The Red Cross man told me I could write a short letter home, and it would be sent through the Red Cross and Allied contacts. I was limited to three or four lines on an official looking form. But at least I could convey to my folks that I was alive and well. I provided no address as the Red Cross representative said my serial number would be sufficient to have it properly delivered. I was glad of that, for as much as I wanted to write, I was concerned about addressing the letter and perhaps providing the Germans with information that they might find useful.

After the shower, clothes and the note, I was taken to one of the separately fenced enclosures and told I was to spend the night in a barracks within the enclosure.

Unbelievably in the enclosure next to mine were two members of my crew: Pappy Derr and Hank Rutkowski. They had waved frantically at me when I first arrived, but all I could do was wave back. We were too far apart to speak to each other. Where were Loel Bishop and Chuck Olson; Don Holmes and Lowell Strain? I knew Joe had died in parachuting, and that, hopefully, Dick Fuller was still hiding out in Holland.

CHAPTER 14

STALAG LUFT I

AT THE END OF THE THIRD DAY, WE WERE taken out of the enclosure and marched down the train track to a line of waiting boxcars. We were crammed into the cars and the heavy side doors were closed and locked. There were so many of us in the car it was impossible for all to sit or lie down. And, in spite of the January cold, stacked together as we were, our collective body heat soon had us sweating. One emaciated looking fellow was sick, or scared to the point of vomit, and the odor triggered several others at my end of the car.

The trip was long, slow, and with many starts and stops. We could see light through the cracks in the car's sides, which provided our only ventilation and a sense of night or day. I know it had been dark outside for some time, when I fell asleep. For the first time in my life, I slept standing up. Exhaustion from weakness had taken over and I slept until light could again be seen through the cracks. There was no telling how far we had traveled, and I had no recollection of how many times we stopped and started.

It is impossible to express in words the horror of that trip. The physical discomfort was extreme and it went on for two days and three nights before the train finally jerked to a halt. Outside we could hear the usual German shouting along with the barking of dogs. The doors of our car were slid open and we tumbled out into the cold but, thank God, fresh air. We formed a miserable looking ragged column and were marched into and through a town. A signpost read "Barth." There were German guards on each side of us with vicious looking barking and snarling police dogs.

The streets of the town were narrow and old and were lined with women, old men and kids. I had one experience I will never forget. One old woman, a grandmoth-erly looking woman, stepped out from the curb as we went by and spat at us and shouted what were probably profanities. I was near the curb and her spit partially caught me in the face. The guard pushed her back to the curb and we continued, but my heart had sunk to a new low. Why me? Why did she spit in my face?

The march was not too far, but in our weakened condi-tion it was far enough. Whenever someone slowed down, a guard would let his dog get close enough to snap at his legs. We helped each other to keep going, two of us supporting a third when necessary. Eventually, we came to a huge fenced-in camp. It appeared to be on a finger of land that had water on both sides. The camp seemed to be made up of several sections, all separately enclosed and with periodic guard towers. Behind the fences were many wooden barracks and along the fence line were hundreds of Allied airmen, British and American. The British looked strange for in spite of their tattered uni-forms, they looked smart and most all wore ties and shirts under their blue tunics. Their mustaches were

long, but I saw no beards. The British airmen undoubtedly had been there for a long, long time. The Americans
looked like Americans. Casual, and not very military.

We were lined up outside what appeared to be the
headquarters building. There was a sign over the gate
leading to the building which read Stalag Luft I, Barth,
Germany. This obviously was to be our home for
probably the duration of the war. Stalag Luft I—the first
and the oldest Luftwaffe "Prisoner of War" camp. It was
a camp for captured Allied air force officers.

All of us were taken, individually, into rooms for
interrogation. The process was long, but there was no
objection to our sitting on the cold ground while waiting
our turn. As usual the interrogators wanted more information than name, rank and serial number. They wanted
family background for some reason. My interrogator
laughed at my stock (name, rank and serial number)
answers, and he looked up my name on his list. He
then told me my home address, my bomb group, and the
location of my base in England. He then asked, "What

was your mother's maiden name?" In exasperation, I said, "Smith," or "Jones." I can't remember which. He laughed again and said, "Try Gleockle." He was right. How did they have all that information? The German intelligence network must be fantastic.

Each of us had our picture taken with an identification number—our kriegie number. Kriegie being our word—it may also be a German word—for prisoner. We received a dog tag with the kriegie number stamped on it. My number was 7386. The dog tag was to be worn at all times.

We were then sorted out. British, Canadian, Australian, and other United Kingdom men were taken off together and we Americans were marched out farther on the finger of land. We were taken to what appeared to be the newest constructed compound. We went through the gates heading towards the barracks area and passed many POW's waiting, watching, and occasionally yelling a greeting to a prior comrade. I was surprised, and oh so pleased, to hear my name called and to see my navigator, Chuck Olson, in the waiting group. When we reached the barracks, we were again divided and we started to fill up a number of empty barracks.

Twenty-four of us were assigned to each room in the barracks. I was in the last group to be assigned and we filled half of our building, which had eight rooms. The rooms had three-level wooden shelves for sleeping along one side and halfway down the other. The shelves were seven to eight feet deep which allowed us to sleep perpendicular to the wall. There was a potbellied stove in the corner on one side, and a long table down the center of the room with benches on each side. There was a small working table by the stove and two glass windows with shutters in the wall at the end of the room. There were two electric light bulbs hanging on wire cords from the ceiling and a loudspeaker mounted over the door.

We had been given a blanket, a tin plate, a cup, and spoon. We also got, courtesy of the Red Cross, a small cardboard parcel with a bar of soap, toothpaste and a toothbrush, and a double-edged safety razor with one blade. I managed to stake my claim for a sleeping spot on the upper level of the longer shelf at the far end. As it turned out, this was an ideal spot to sit for hours leaning against the wall writing, reading, and generally whiling away the interminable hours.

Shortly after the twenty-four of us were established in our room, the Germans left. We were, seemingly, left on our own. Fortunately, this was not the case, as a couple of fellows came in to welcome us to our brand new home. One was a major and the other a captain. They explained how life was in the compound. What the rules were. How, laughingly, we were to be fed, and so on and so on. It appeared we were well organized internally and the American and British compounds were under the command of the camp's ranking officer, Colonel Zemke. He was a well-known American fighter pilot, an "ace" with twenty-eight kills to his credit, who had finally run out of luck. The next in command was Lt. Colonel Gabreski.

We had to find our ranking officer to be in charge of our group. We had 2nd and 1st Lieutenants, and the 1st Lieutenant with the most seniority, like it or not, got the job. We also had to elect a couple of cooks to make all kinds of goodies out of "ersatz" bread (which was primarily sawdust), rutabagas (a regular staple), and whatever else ingenuity could provide. We were told that once a day we were allowed to get drinking water. Four pails were provided, and we were to send two men to get the water. Once a day, we were to send two men to the German cook shed to pick up two pails of soup that occasionally had solid vegetables in the broth. With experience, we learned to try and obtain a position in the line at the cook shed so that our pails would be filled from the bottom of the large kettles used to make the soup. Taken from near the bottom, the soup would contain less broth and more solids. As time passed and we all became weaker from hunger, the water detail became quite a chore. The water detail ended up with two men carrying one bucket and making several trips. We also learned, from our advisors, how the war was progressing. There were radios in the camp made by inventive Yankees, and the war news was delivered daily by one designated officer to avoid false rumors. At this point, the war news was great. The Russians were continuing their advance, and the Battle of the Bulge was being, or had been, contained. We were told that the loudspeaker in the room was used by the Germans to make announcements, to issue orders, and spread their propaganda.

CHAPTER 15

THE REUNION

AS SOON AS I WAS ABLE, I LEFT THE BARRACKS
to look for Chuck. I found him in his barracks, which was
next to mine. I was surprised to learn that he was the last
to parachute from the ship. I had assumed that Dick and
I were the last, but Chuck, never known for his speed or
organization, had forgotten something and had gone
back to his station to retrieve whatever it was. He then
decided he didn't want to jump from the small escape
hatch in the nose of the plane, and casually went back to
the open bomb bay. He then realized he was all alone, and
quickly exited. I recalled seeing what I thought might be

a parachute, as I watched, from my own chute, our B-17 heading for the ground. It must have been Chuck. He had been picked up immediately on his landing and had no chance to escape. I told Chuck about seeing others of our crew at Dulag Luft and about Joe whom we lost, and Dick, who, with luck, might still be free in Holland.

Several days later, word spread through the camp that more kriegies were coming. We went out to the fence to see the new group come in. Unbelievably, in the group of all enlisted men and non-coms (non-commissioned officers), were my two crewmembers from Dulag Luft. It seems that the Geneva Convention after World War I, determined that all POW officers should have orderlies. The Swiss Red Cross, which tried to oversee POW operations, periodically reminded the Germans of this requirement. The Germans would then send a contingent of enlisted men to officer camps. Pappy Derr had heard of this and he and Hank had volunteered to be orderlies. Pappy knew that no member of a flight crew would have to work as an orderly in an American Air Corps compound and the alternative was probably hard work and poorer treatment in a regular prison camp.

As soon as the newcomers were assigned to a barracks, Chuck and I rushed over to see them. Pappy and Hank had managed to stay together and were assigned to the same room in the barracks. We compared notes and learned that Bish had been the first out, and had landed on the outskirts of town and was able, with help, to escape capture. Dick, Chuck, and I had landed away from town, and only Chuck had been immediately picked up. Chuck's quick capture was why he had been the first to arrive at Stalag Luft I.

Pappy and Hank now brought us up to date about their capture along with my top turret and ball turret gunners. They all bailed out of the plane, one after another, shortly after Bish who was first and who had disappeared in the clouds. They landed fairly close together near what looked like the edge of a town. They later learned that they were just outside the city of Meppel.

They were helping each other to get free from their

parachutes when a group of German soldiers headed for them in a military truck. The Germans shoved them on to the truck and took them back into the city. They ended up at a large warehouse and were taken inside and placed in individual cages. (Cages is what Hank Rutkowski called the individual cells.)

A day or so later they were taken by truck to another town and another military jail. The next day they were taken across the border and into Germany. After several transfers they arrived in the Germans' "Dulag Luft." There, the four stayed as regular prisoners, until Pappy and Hank were transferred here. "Here," in "Stalag Luft 1."

It is still hard to believe that most of my crew were initially close together after bailing out of the plane. I had no knowledge of where they all were until now. Anyway, here in Stalag Luft 1, four of us were together.

CHAPTER 16

LIFE IN POW CAMP

THE DAYS AND THE WEEKS CONTINUE TO wear on. I try to keep busy by writing this log of my "adventure," and by attending a variety of school-type classes given by whatever experts we have in the compound. Food, flying, and girls are the usual topics of conversation, and in that order of importance. It seems that no matter what is being discussed, the subject always comes back to food. We are all so hungry.

Occasionally, the word would spread wildly that there was a delivery of Red Cross parcels. Each parcel contained small cans of food, powdered milk, a pack of cigarettes, a chocolate bar, and toothpaste and soap. The parcel is planned for one man per parcel per week. We usually get one parcel for twenty-four men, infrequently. It is absolutely amazing what our cooks can do with practically nothing. By using toothpaste as a baking powder, they can bake cookies made out of ersatz bread and chocolate. One favorite of mine is a breakfast cereal that occasionally we have on a Sunday morning. It is made from one-quarter-inch size cubes of the ersatz bread, toasted, and served with the powdered milk. We write these recipes down in little blue notebooks that come in the Red Cross parcels. My little books, I have two, contain lists of favorite restaurants all over the United States, plans for meals to be prepared when we are home again, the menu of our Easter dinner that we made from the same old stuff but with additional inge-nuity, and the menu we plan for our victory dinner when victory eventually comes. There are other personal things in our books plus the names and addresses of our new twenty-four close associates.

The inside fence around the camp is low enough to be climbed, but it is only the inside boundary of a "no-man" strip about twenty yards wide. A high barbed wire fence with guard towers surrounds the inner fence and the "no-man" strip. There is a simple and enforced rule. No one, for any reason, can enter the strip. The guards in the towers have orders to shoot first and question later. It had happened in the past, and our commanding officers made sure that we all understood the rule and didn't commit suicide by retrieving a wayward soccer or baseball. The guards periodically throw such things back into the compound.

From our compound, the farthest out on the peninsula, there appears no way to escape, especially over or under the fences. There is water on three sides, and miles of compounds and fencing on the narrow side towards the mainland. The "honey wagon," which is a two-wheel wooden cart pulled by an old horse, is used to carry out the sewage from the latrines. It might provide transportation through the gates if anyone could stomach crawling into the wagon under its obnoxious cargo. To my knowledge no one ever tried that smelly and doubtful route to freedom.

Occasionally we are required to leave the barracks while the guards search our quarters. This is generally a room-to-room search and the timing is quite at random. It starts with a lot of whistle blowing and guards bursting into rooms. What they are looking for, I really don't know, but I do worry about the guards finding and confiscating my notes for this "adventure" story. I have been very careful about not writing down any names, places or anything else that would compromise my Dutch contacts. I imagine the guards probably cannot read English, but I'm not taking any chances.

The guards are very interested in the map of Europe we have tacked to the back of our door. When we receive our daily news briefing, from our own people, we mark on the map the steady advance of the Allied forces into Germany. The guards study our map so intently, it's obvious they are not getting the same information from German sources. Every room has its own "war" map and all have the same information, giving credence to what the Germans have to believe is true.

There was one exceptionally frightening experience that each of us shared in our hearts. One day, the Germans stormed into our room and asked for one of the boys who had a Jewish name. No explanation. They just said, "Get *your things, and come with us." We heard later that he was taken, along with other Americans with Jewish names, and put in a separate compound. He was terrified at the time, and so were we, for he was a great guy and lots of fun. We felt sure he and the others would be shipped off to one of the Jewish concentration camps we had started to hear about.*

The winter months were hard. Our room was never warm. Our coal supply was meager. One or two bricks of powdered coal per day was the ration to be used for heat and for any cooking we tried to do. Most of the evenings, we just wrapped ourselves in our blankets and watched the flickering candles of our "kriegie" lamps. The electric lights were turned off early, and we made the candle lamps out of tin cans. The candles were provided by the Germans, probably due to Red Cross prodding.

Spring is coming now, and the weather is warming. My toes still throb with frostbite and my gums continue to bleed whenever I bite into anything. Probably, some day, my teeth will fall out. My clothes seem to be getting bigger in spite of their shrinking after our recent visit to the de-lousing building. There we had a one-minute hot, one-minute cold, shower while our clothes were deloused in a steamer. It was nice to feel somewhat clean and to get rid of the little white bugs that had infested our clothes.

I am going to close now. I've lost interest in my "adventure" project. It just seems to go on, and on, and on. There is hope in sight, but it's tough to keep from being depressed. I can only pray that someday I will be free and home again.

NO BOOK OF REFLECTIONS COMPILED FROM the cryptic notes made in Stalag Luft I should just come to an end. I, being the author, obviously survived. So let me bring my story to a more satisfactory ending.

As the war in Europe drew to a close, the Russians were pressing toward Berlin from the east, and the British and American troops from the west. It was a toss-up as to whether the British or the Russians would reach our camp first. We were leery of the Russians, and would prefer to see the British first. Unfortunately, the British advance slowed near Lubeck while the Russian advance continued and it appeared that they would probably be our liberators. Our Luftwaffe guards had been replaced by Wehrmacht GI's. And as things got tougher for the Germans, and they could see the writing on the wall, the Wehrmacht also disappeared and the Home Guard took over the camp. The Home Guard were elderly men with bits and pieces of uniforms. Some wore only army hats. Their weapons were antiquated rifles, which probably hadn't been fired in many years.

Escape at this time would have been possible, but where would one go with warring factions all around? It was better to sit tight a short while more. We were no longer needed by our country. We were just emaciated "has-beens."

One morning in late April, we were awakened by the blasting of American band music from our room speaker. Then came the announcement by one of our officers telling us that all the Germans had left the camp during the night, and the Russians were practically at our gate. Colonel Zemke, with his staff, had gone to meet them to avoid any problems. We were told to stay put, and stay together. But, for us, our kriegie days were over. You can imagine the cheering. The noise from the camp was probably heard in Berlin.

Shortly thereafter, the war was officially over, and word finally came that we would be flown out from the Barth airport as soon as it could be arranged. We would be taken to debarkation camps and from there to the good old USA. There was one catch. The Russians insisted that each POW have a passport before they would allow him to leave the camp. What an absurd requirement. It was going to hold up our leaving for quite some time, and a number of fellows just took off to work their own way back to more friendly territory.

The Russians had brought in several truckloads of potatoes—ours for the taking. They also brought in a herd of cows, and ex-kriegies with butchering experience got to work. I filled up a mop pail with potatoes and boiled them over one of the many cooking fires that were built all over the compound. The one I used was fueled by burning the end of a telephone pole. I ate the whole pailfull of potatoes. Just plain. No salt. Nothing. Boy, did they taste good, but did I ever get sick! We had meat after a while when our resident butchers broke down the herd to manageable size pieces.

An interesting phenomenon was occurring. We had been, for a long time, tightly confined and with absolutely no privacy. Now we seemed to need some sort of individual space. So, springing up all over, were private or semi-private outhouses. These private "johns" were being built, by ex-Kriegies outside the fencing and on the bluffs overlooking the Baltic Sea.

Freedom became all the more meaningful to us as we discovered out on the bluffs a series of small bunker type cells. They were large enough for probably a half dozen people. Each had a barred gate entrance with a steel outer door. When the door was closed it completely covered the gate and prevented air from entering the cell. On the top of the bunkers were what appeared to be air tubes that could be capped off. The consensus of those of us inspecting the cells was that they were small gas chambers to provide the Germans with a quiet way of dispensing any unwanted prisoners. I didn't know if this was true, but it was a horrible thought.

We were able to go into town, but our command warned us to never go alone, and to avoid contact with the Russians. They were, it seemed, unpredictable. They had arrived like a migrating horde with no noticeable organization. They came on foot, on horseback, in trucks, on motorcycles. They just came, living off the land.

They did provide us entertainment. I remember one afternoon, a group of Russian musicians and dancers put on an exciting program of Russian dances. There were Russian women in Cossack costumes, and after the program, they changed into their army uniforms and left with their weapons slung over their shoulders.

On one trip to town, an elderly German man contacted me. He spoke reasonable English, and he seemed to have items in his house for sale. I looked at his wares, and there was a pair of Royal Air Force fleece-lined flying boots, practically new and just my size. I bought the boots for a pack of cigarettes and wore them back to the compound. I managed to hang on to those boots and used them in winter for many years. At one time they were even used to add authenticity to the Santa Claus costume at a Christmas party for underprivileged kids.

There was a rumor circulating, which I personally cannot confirm. The word was that there was an underground factory manned by French, Polish and other political prisoners beneath the Barth airfield. The people in town knew of the factory but were afraid to tell the Russians. They were just going to leave the workers locked in to probably die. Fortunately, the factory was discovered and the emaciated workers released.

After a couple of weeks of waiting, we were flown out of Germany by B-17s supplied from the various groups in the Eighth Air Force. We were flown low over German cities, so we could see the havoc our bombs had done, and then on to the French coast to "re-claimed Allied military camps." My camp was named "Camp Lucky Strike." After a period of time, during which we were carefully fed easily digested foods, and issued new Class A uniforms, we were boarded on ships and on to home.

Tired of the waiting for our ship, a friend and I slipped

out of camp and hitchhiked to Paris for a few days. After all we had been through, we were not going to leave Europe without at least seeing Paris. It was a great few days. We had heard through the GI grapevine that we could trade cigarettes for cash, or we could simply show up at a headquarters building, as newly arrived ex-prisoners, and receive an advance on our back pay. This we did, and as an added bonus we were outfitted again with new uniforms.

The downside happened when we returned to Lucky Strike and found our barrack bags sitting on top of our cots in an otherwise empty tent. It seemed that while we were gone, everyone else in our tent, which was huge and held several dozen people, had been transferred to a ship bound for the USA. What to do? We just moved our possessions to another tent that was being filled with new "re-claimed Allied military personnel" that were arriving daily. We then left on the next ship for home.

As soon as I could, I contacted my folks by phone. They were alive and well. The Army, with considerable compassion, did not send MIA telegrams to "next of kin" over the Christmas season, so my status did not completely ruin their holiday. My prayers had been answered.

My folks did receive the short note I was allowed to write back in Dulag Luft. But, better yet, my name along with many others was read over shortwave radio by the Swiss Red Cross, and my parents heard from several people, from all parts of the United States, that I was alive and a POW in a German camp.

My very good friend, from boyhood and college, Lt. Roy Brockman, also a B-17 pilot in the Eighth Air Force, flew into my base in England for a visit the day I did not return from my fateful mission. He saw my name on the operations board as a casualty with unknown status. Wisely, Roy kept this information under his hat and did not inform anyone back home until it was known that I was alive and a POW.

Back in the States, I made contact with officials in Meppel, Holland to learn what I could about my heroic Dutch friends. Absolutely unbelievably, I learned that on Christmas Eve, the night following the afternoon Bish and I were taken from the Meppel City jail, a resistance force broke into the jail and rescued Peter and Mimi. They got them out of town and to a safe haven where they recuperated. One Dutch Policeman was killed in the raid, probably the only German collaborator on the force. Peter took over his command of the area resistance force and eventually helped liberate Meppel. He subsequently was awarded medals for all his resistance work from General Eisenhower and his Queen, Wilhelmina.

Additional wonderful news—Mientje was also alive and well. She survived an internment camp and was freed by Allied troops.

Other news. Bish had been sent from Dulag Luft to an internment camp for enlisted airmen, and now was back in the USA. So were the rest of my crew and we all were in contact by telephone. I made "off and on" visits to Pappy in Pennsylvania, and to Chuck in New Jersey. I also was Chuck's best man at his marriage in New York City. Dick Fuller, my co-pilot, was back in California. I've yet to find out how he got out of Meppel, unless it was after the war.

Remember the old man who watched my plane head

into the earth? Actually, the plane had crashed into a small lake that since has been included in a chain of man-made lakes along Holland's coast. He had told his grandson, Rint, about the plane many times. Some 40 years later, Rint, now a prominent building contractor in Meppel and an avid scuba diver, located my plane. He was able to retrieve several mementos from the plane that was almost entirely buried in mud in the bottom of the lake. He obtained the manufacturer's nameplate from the cockpit, and the pilot's oxygen mask. I made my third trip to Holland to meet this gentleman, along with Peter, Mimi, Mientje, and others, and he took me out on his cabin cruiser to the middle of the lake and stopped the boat. He then told me I was right above my B-17, and with flair, he presented me with the nameplate and my old oxygen mask. His wife, Janny and Peter took pictures. The pictures and an account of my wartime stay in Meppel all ended up in the Meppel newspaper. The mayor of Meppel even presented me with a commemorative tie, which I prize highly and wear on special occasions.

The newspaper article had an unexpected and very

welcome result. Two of the boys who helped me, when I first landed in that wet field on December 6, 1944, were brothers. They read the newspaper article, obtained my home address, wrote to me, and since then we have corresponded several times. It was in their family home where I waited by that potbelly stove for Mimi, who was my first contact with the Dutch Resistance. The boys, obviously now men of about my age, sent me a photograph of their family as it was in 1944, and pictures of the field where we first made contact and the wooded area where we waited for the cover of darkness. I also learned that their sister was one of the young ladies who brought me the Dutch clothing to replace my uniform. I hope, someday soon, to meet them face to face and to thank them again for their courageous help so many years ago.

AUTHOR'S NOTE AND
ACKNOWLEDGMENTS

BEHIND ENEMY LINES HAS BEEN WRITTEN to record the heroism of the Dutch people who assisted me when I parachuted into German occupied Holland on December 6, 1944.

The book is based on fact as far as I can recall, using notes I made back in 1945. The names of my B-17 bomber crew are real. The full names of my Dutch "Helpers" are either unknown or intentionally omitted.

I want to express my gratitude to my wife Nancy, who encouraged my writing *Behind Enemy Lines,* and for her assistance in the editing of the text. I also want to thank my sons, their wives and other friends for their assistance. To my son Doug, I owe special thanks for his patient responses to my late night phone calls for help in solving my seemingly endless computer problems in establishing the text in its final printed form.

H. R. DeMallie

ABOUT THE AUTHOR

HOWARD R. DEMALLIE was born in Rochester, New York. Ironically, his grandfather was from Holland, the country whose people helped Mr. DeMallie after he parachuted from his B17 bomber. After the war he returned to the University of Michigan and graduated with a degree in engineering. He settled in Rochester where he worked for Eastman Kodak and became the Director of Engineering for film machine design. He is a holder of seven patents on film slitting, spooling, and packaging technology.

Mr. DeMallie has two sons and is now retired and lives in Rochester with his wife Nancy.

Mr. DeMallie wrote this book to record his remarkable experiences during World War II and to pay tribute to the brave Dutch people who risked their lives to help him and his crewmates after his plane was shot down over Holland. He continues to stay in touch with some of those people and to participate in the Air Force Escape and Invasion Society.

BOOKS IN THIS SERIES

✹STERLING POINT BOOKS